The Complete Budgeting Guide

From Debt Reduction to Savings Building

Brittney Mann

Table of Contents

INTRODUCTION

If the word budget makes you cringe, you're reading the right book. Old-style personal financial advice equates budgeting with constant expense tracking, deep cost-cutting (mostly of all the fun stuff), and a lot of math. It sounds boring and frustrating, and no one (including me) wants to do it.

The truth is that budgeting doesn't mean sacrifice; it means choice. A budget is a plan for your money that will let you take control of your finances so that you can have all of the things that you want, whatever they are. You can gear your budget toward the life you want, whether that includes ironclad financial security, the freedom to ditch your job and travel the world, or resources to buy your dream house and start a family.

Budgeting is about designing a road map to financial security and prosperity. Sometimes that path includes cutting back on expenses (especially the ones that aren't bringing you any benefits); other times it creates space for major life changes (like buying a house). It's a way to tap into your resources wisely and transform them into future wealth.

More than all of that, it's a way to take the anxiety out of money management: instead of stressing over every bill that comes in, for example, you'll already have figured out exactly how to pay it. You'll have a plan for eliminating the debt that's been keeping you up at night. You won't have to worry about whether or not you'll have enough money to fund your retirement. That financial confidence will help you overcome the challenges that have been keeping you from getting ahead and accumulating a healthy nest egg.

To get to the financial destination you want, though, you need to know where you're starting from. You'll use that information to set a course that will help you reach your goals. Your budget will act as the GPS, giving you directions and rerouting you when detours pop up so you can get wherever you want to go.

Chapter 1
Budgeting Basics

Most people have the wrong idea about budgets. They think they're all about eating no-brand ramen noodles in the dark to save money and keeping endlessly detailed records of every penny spent. The real point of a budget is to make sure you're never in a position where ramen noodles are all you can afford to eat or you're praying your power doesn't get shut off because you couldn't pay the bill.

In this chapter, we'll expose budgeting myths, take a look at budget reality, and reveal the best way to make this personalized money plan work for you. With this powerful tool, you'll be able to build wealth, meet and exceed your goals, and be ready whenever unexpected financial setbacks occur.

WHAT BUDGETING IS (AND ISN'T)

A Money Plan . . . Not a Magic Potion

The right budget is a game plan for your money that assigns specific jobs to every dollar, whether that job is to pay the electric bill, buy this week's groceries, or beef up your 401(k) account. That plan helps you direct cash toward your financial goals, from paying cash for your next car to funding a destination wedding to enjoying a stress-free retirement. A budget lets you decide ahead of time what you want to do with your money instead of spending randomly in ways that undermine your plans and leave you with a mountain of debt.

What budgeting won't do is magically and instantly solve all of your money problems. It's not a quick fix or a perfect formula. But with time and focus it can move you out of a monthly money crunch and toward financial freedom and prosperity.

A Small Leather Bag

The word budget comes to us from fifteenth-century France, where a bougette was a little leather bag or pouch that was used to carry money (sort of like a wallet). After a hundred years or so, the word morphed into budget and began to refer to the money inside the pouch.

Bottom line: a budget tailored to your life—as opposed to your life tailored to a budget—can help you spend consciously, dig out of debt, and build substantial wealth.

BUSTING BUDGET MYTHS

There are many misconceptions about budgets floating around, and they keep a lot of people from taking control of their money. Don't let these myths get in the way of your financial future. We'll knock down these false obstacles so you can feel good about creating your money plan.

- **Myth: Budgets are for other people.** Truth: Everyone can benefit from a budget. Paying attention to your finances is the best way to avoid crippling debt and build lasting wealth.

- **Myth: Budgets are too stressful.** Truth: Running out of money every month before your bills are paid, being stuck in debt, and having little or no savings causes anxiety. Budgeting so you can manage your money better will reduce your stress.

- **Myth: Budgets need to be highly detailed.** Truth: That's up to you. You can zoom in and look at each separate line item or zoom out and look at high-level income and expense buckets.

- **Myth: Budgets mean cutting back on fun.** Truth: You won't feel cutbacks in a budget that's right for you. Yes, you may end up trimming some expenses, but that's your choice —and it's not the only way to reach your financial goals. Budgeting doesn't mean restricting spending; it means spending money on the right things.

- **Myth: Going over budget blows up everything.** Truth: Going over budget is like eating a donut when you're on a diet. Sure, it's a mistake, but it doesn't erase everything else you've been doing. Budgets are flexible, and they grow and change to reflect your needs. Give yourself a break, and do what you can to get back on track.

- **Myth: Budgets are time hogs.** Truth: You can make your budget as time-consuming as you want, including not at all. If you can't (or don't want to) spend time budgeting, work with an app that automatically tracks and updates for you and even lets you set up alerts to keep you from going over budget.

Here's the real deal: creating your first budget takes a little work and some time, even if you're going fully automated with an app. Once that's done, following the budget takes nothing but some thought and commitment. Even if you're not totally ready to stick to a budget, make it anyway. You'll be surprised how much easier it is to deal with your money.

RICH PEOPLE ALWAYS BUDGET

Making a lot of money and having a lot of money aren't the same thing. The people you might think are rich because of their giant mansions and stable of sports cars often face the same money struggles as people living paycheck to paycheck. Their lives are focused on conspicuous consumption, and they're often deep in debt to finance their "rich" lifestyle.

The Royal Budget

Back in the nineteenth century, only the very rich used household budgets. In fact, some of the earliest historical mentions came from diaries of the royal households of Europe. Kings and princes tracked their holdings and their spending to make sure their wealth wouldn't decline.

People who are in great financial shape—regardless of their income—got there (and stay there) by budgeting. In fact, you'd be hard-pressed to find an individual with a high net worth who didn't know exactly where his or her money was going. That doesn't mean wealthy people count pennies and track lattes; it just means that they have a plan for their money and are following it. They focus more on saving and investing than on spending to make sure they never go over budget.

THE TRUTH ABOUT TRACKING

If you wonder why there's never enough money to get you through the month, there's a simple way to find out: track your spending. Knowing exactly what you're spending money on is the best way to sniff out mindless money habits (and we all have them).

You'll probably be surprised when you see your spending laid out in front of you, but at least you'll have a crystal-clear picture of where your money really went and not just where you thought it went. For example, you might think you spend $400 a month on groceries when you're really spending $600. If you only budget for that $400 estimate, you're destined to have a budget failure. This will also capture things you didn't even realize you were spending—or overspending—money on, like an old subscription you never thought to cancel.

To track your money, write down or digitally capture every dollar you spend for one month. Include everything, from your $1,800 mortgage payment to the $4 coffee you grabbed on your way into work. Here, savings counts as an expense, so remember to include any money you put into a savings or retirement account (unless it was taken out of your paycheck— don't include that). Record each expense regardless of whether you pay by cash, check, debit or credit card, automatic payment, or online transfer.

Now you can see where your money is really going and where you're unintentionally overspending. With that information laid out in front of you, you can decide whether you want to redirect some of that cash in your budget. And that's the beauty of budgeting: it gives you the power to choose what you want to do with your money instead of reacting after it's already gone.

BREAK OUT OF THE PAYCHECK-TO-PAYCHECK CYCLE

One of the main benefits budgeting brings is busting you out of damaging financial cycles, like living paycheck to paycheck. Millions of people—including high earners—live paycheck to paycheck every month, meaning they have no money other than their upcoming take-home pay to count on. That situation makes it impossible to save money and build wealth, and it traps you exactly where you are whether you like it or not. You can't change jobs or move to a new city, for example, when you're always biting your nails waiting for that next paycheck.

If you're stuck in this situation, you're probably turning to credit cards to cover some of your monthly expenses, which makes it even harder to cover next month's bills. You are always one emergency away from financial disaster. That constant financial struggle can wreak havoc on your plans and your stress levels. Budgeting can change that.

The way out of the paycheck-to-paycheck problem is to acknowledge it and make some hard temporary changes to your spending. Breaking out of this destructive cycle is difficult, but creating and sticking to a budget will help get you out of it. Once you're free, there will be room in your budget to build substantial savings, and from there you can turn toward accumulating wealth.

USING YOUR BUDGET TO CREATE WEALTH

Your Very Own "Get Rich" Scheme

The real purpose of a budget is to help you take control of your finances and create personal wealth. That's why multinational corporations and millionaires (and billionaires) alike use them as blueprints to bring in more income and build bigger fortunes. The trick is in how they put their money to work, using shrewd investment strategies to grow that money faster.

This budget focus comes after you've paid off all of your debt (other than an affordable mortgage) and have a good handle on spending less than you earn. That's because you'll almost always pay more interest on debt than you will earn by investing—a net loss to your overall finances. Once you're debt-free, you can divert some or all of those retired loan payments toward the future.

Saving and Investing Are Not the Same

People use the terms saving and investing interchangeably, but they're not the same thing. Saving means accumulating cash in a secure space where there's no risk of loss; it's money you can count on 100 percent. Investing involves buying something with the hope that it will increase in value and accepting the possibility that it might decrease in value or even become completely worthless.

Accumulating money is just the first part of the plan, and you can build up a tidy nest egg with pure savings. But if you also carefully invest some of your money, you can begin to build serious wealth.

FOCUS FIRST ON SAVING

When you're consciously directing your dollars, you can send them exactly where you want them to go. By purposefully putting more money into saving, rather than spending on things you don't really need, you'll see your wealth grow consistently. As Warren Buffett says, "Do not save what is left after spending; instead spend what is left after saving." In time, this strategy will lead to substantially more financial freedom and opportunity.

Saving guarantees that you'll have money when you need it. Every dollar you put into savings is a dollar you will definitely get back. In exchange for that security, the interest you'll earn on savings is generally pretty low; it's the trade-off for guaranteed safety.

With a focus on savings, you'll be able to build up some cash reserves, including enough cash to begin investing with. Once you've taken advantage of employer-based retirement savings (more on that in Chapter 3), you can begin to build savings to meet your goals, from creating an emergency fund to saving for a down payment on a house. Tools like the Qapital app are designed for exactly that: helping you automatically direct your money toward specific goals based on your settings. For example, you can direct the Qapital app to round up to the nearest dollar every time you spend money, with the rounding amount moved into the target savings account.

START INVESTING YOUR MONEY

Most people's first experience with investing comes when they have to pick 401(k) funds at work. If you don't know much about investing, getting started can seem intimidating. Figuring out how to choose among millions of investments can be so daunting that it makes you choose no investment at all. And if you've lived through a sharp market downturn (stock or housing, for example), the fear of losses can keep you from seizing potentially profitable opportunities. That's why it's important to only invest money you can afford (but don't expect) to lose and to understand every investment you make. A good way to wade into investing is to start with exchange-traded funds (ETFs) or index mutual funds; both offer you the chance to hold an entire portfolio of investments in a single share, and they're among the most cost-effective (low-fee) investment options.

Investing versus Trading

Investing is a long-term proposition, where you buy an asset (like a stock or a house) that has the potential to grow substantially over time. Trading is more like gambling, where you try to guess what's going to happen on any given day—and you'll usually guess wrong. Investing is about building wealth. Trading is about the thrill of the ride.

If you're itching to start investing but don't have a sizeable stash to contribute all at once, take advantage of beginner investing platforms, such as Swell Investing or apps like Acorns that let you consistently automatically funnel very small amounts of money ($1 here, $5 there) into investing. This strategy is called microinvesting. Those small amounts very quickly grow into substantial portfolios that will help you reach your financial goals in no time.

Build an Empire of Assets

The key to true wealth is putting your money to work for you. Practically speaking, that means spending money on income-producing assets that will supply cash and continue to grow in value over time. The most common assets used to build wealth include:

- Stocks
- Bonds
- Real estate

Of course, as with any investment, there's always the risk of declining value or even total loss. Carefully choosing and diversifying assets (holding several different kinds) can greatly reduce the risk that you'll lose everything and increase your opportunities for long-term financial income and growth.

SETTING YOUR FINANCIAL GOALS

How to Get Everything You Want

To create a budget that will help you meet your goals, you first have to figure out what your goals are and define them. This step will help you see and measure your progress, allowing you to make any necessary adjustments along the way. The key here is to think SMART:

- **S**pecific
- **M**easurable
- **A**chievable
- **R**ealistic
- **T**ime-oriented

Framing your goals this way gives you a much better shot at reaching them and continuing forward financially.

Start by coming up with three SMART goals, and make sure to write them down. According to research, the simple act of writing down your goals makes you much more likely to achieve them.

GET SPECIFIC

When you're thinking about your goals, make them crystal clear. Saying "I want to be rich," for example, won't get you there. But add some specifics to that idea, like "I want to have

$1 million in my retirement account," and you're already starting on your way.

Think about the things you want to do with your money, and add explicit details to turn those general ideas into specific goals with definite dollar amounts. Here are some examples of transforming ideas into goals:

- "A car" becomes "Buy a used Subaru Outback for $8,000."
- "A vacation" becomes "Take a two-week trip to the Italian Riviera next summer for $3,500 by staying in an Airbnb."
- "Retire early" becomes "Create a $1,500,000 nest egg so I can stop working by the time I hit 50."

Adding these vivid details helps bring your goals to life, making them feel more like something you really can do. You can more clearly see where they stand now financially, how much more you'll need to save, and how long it will take you to meet them.

TAKING MEASURE

Without a clear way to measure your progress, it's easy to get frustrated and give up on your goals. When you make your goals measurable ("save $1,000 in my emergency fund"), you can see every step that takes you closer, and those steps feel like small victories.

Measuring also helps you stay motivated. Whether you carve your goal into a series of more quickly reachable minigoals (cheering every $100 on the way to $1,000) or make yourself a visual (like the color-in thermometer signs that charities use), active measuring will keep you on track and excited about hitting your targets.

That doesn't mean you should check in every day. Measuring too often can be frustrating because the progress seems to move at a snail's pace. Figure out reasonable checkin periods based on your budget so you can see significant changes. For example, if you're saving $50 a month toward a $1,000 goal, checking in every three months will give you a better boost than checking in more often would.

ACHIEVABLE AND REALISTIC

In order to meet your goals, they have to be possible—and that means both achievable and realistic. If they're not, you'll fail to meet them, and that can quickly derail your motivation and undermine your financial future.

Here, achievable and realistic mean workable within your budget. While it's not possible to save $30,000 in one year when you're earning $25,000, you can set an achievable goal of saving $1,000. Maybe putting away $100 a month wouldn't be realistic in your situation, but banking $85 is something you can do. Make sure the goals you set can fit into your budget without crowding out any necessities.

As you begin to bring in more money and work to control unnecessary spending, you'll free up even more space in your budget. That will allow you to set bigger goals that you'll have no trouble reaching.

SET A TIME FRAME

Time is another key factor in goal setting and tracking. For one thing, it sets the clock running, which will encourage you to get moving. In addition, the time frame may affect your goal-reaching strategy.

Let's start with the tracking point. It's harder to gauge an open-ended goal than one with a clear end point. With a clear time frame ("save $1,000 in four months"), you can easily see what you need to do to reach your goal (save $250 a month). Remove the time frame ("save $1,000"), though, and your goal seems less urgent and easier to ignore. Locking in a time frame also adds a motivation factor. Working to a deadline forces you to get the job done by regularly taking the steps you need to meet your goal.

The Scoop on IRAs

IRAs are individual retirement accounts, and there are two main types: traditional and Roth. Traditional IRAs give you a current tax deduction and let your money grow tax-deferred; you don't pay any taxes until you start pulling money out. Roth IRAs start with after-tax money (no deduction now), and let your money grow tax-free; you won't pay tax on any of the earnings or future withdrawals.

Then there's the path to reach your goal. For short-term goals, less than three years away (maybe buying a car or going to Mardi Gras), you want to keep your money somewhere completely risk-free, like a savings account. For longer-term goals, like saving for retirement or for your kids' college, you have more flexibility and more time to recover from potential setbacks. That gives you the opportunity to invest at least a portion of the money you're putting toward that goal and let compounding do part of the work to move you closer to meeting it.

BREAK GOALS DOWN INTO STEPS

Once you have your SMART goals written down, figure out what steps you need to take in order to meet them. Listing those steps offers you a framework to follow so you'll actually get started and stay on track.

For example, if your goal is to save $5,000 toward retirement this year, your steps might include things like "open a Roth IRA account" and "set up weekly automatic $100 transfers into the IRA." If your goal is to work on paying down your student loans, steps might include "verify my student loan balance" and "look into alternative repayment plans."

Cross off each step as you accomplish it and each minigoal as you meet it. That might sound silly, but studies show that the act of marking things as done releases positive brain chemicals, sort of like winning a prize. The more good feelings your brain associates with your goals, the more you'll want to keep going.

KNOW YOUR PRIORITIES

Would You Rather . . .

You know what's most important to you, and you can create your budget to reflect your financial priorities. For example, if buying your dream house is more important to you than saving for retirement, saving up a down payment will take a higher priority in your plans than 401(k) contributions. That doesn't mean you can't do both but rather that you'll budget for money going into the "house account" before you budget extra money for retirement savings.

Keep in mind that some financial goals can help pave the way for others. For example, paying off high-interest debt will make it easier to save up for a down payment. Not only will the payoff free up space in your budget, it will also reduce the amount of interest you would have had to pay, which means even more money toward your house goal. Plus, debt repayment has the added effect of improving your credit score, which can get you a better interest rate when you get a mortgage.

If you've never really thought about things like this before, using prompts can help. Websites like www.smartaboutmoney.org offer all sorts of worksheets, tools, and quizzes to get you started and help clarify your financial priorities.

RANK YOUR GOALS

Now that your SMART goals are set, you'll decide which are the most important to you and to your financial future. Those will be the highest-ranked goals, taking top priority in your budget.

Try to think financially rather than emotionally as you rank your goals. It's natural to prefer working on fun things (like vacations) to burdens (like credit card debt). But paying down your credit card debt as the first priority will help you get to your vacation without the shadow of even more debt hanging over your fun.

How Do Your Goals Stack Up?

According to a 2017 survey by NerdWallet, 89 percent of Americans have financial goals. Paying down debt scored the top rank (58 percent), followed by general savings (53 percent), avoiding new debt (42 percent), saving for vacation (31 percent), and starting or increasing retirement savings contributions (28 percent).

To keep yourself motivated through chore-type goals (like paying off student loans) until you make it to more pleasurable goals (like spending a year in Paris), use the fun goals as your incentive. For example, tell yourself that "After my student loans are paid off, I can start saving for my year in Paris." By connecting the two goals (also called stacking goals), the higher priority chore-type goal will start to feel less like a burden and more like a gateway to what you really want.

SET THE TIMELINE

Now that you've prioritized your goals, sort them into time-based categories: short-term, mid-term, and long-term. Short-term priorities take place within two to three years. These might include things like saving up for a new laptop so you can start freelance writing or going on a family vacation over the holidays. Mid-term priorities are three to five years out from now and could include things like replacing the car you're driving now or remodeling your kitchen. Anything further off than five years fits in the long-term category. That's for priorities like paying off your mortgage or enjoying your dream retirement.

Putting your priorities on a timeline lets you save for all three categories at once, but in different ways. For short-term priorities, you need risk-free, easy-access cash. That means putting the money you're saving toward those priorities in regular savings accounts or money market accounts that are insured by the Federal Deposit Insurance Corporation (FDIC). You won't earn much interest, but your money will be safe and there won't be any penalties when you take it out. For your mid-term priorities, you still want to stick with risk-free or very low-risk places to park your money, but you have a little more time to play with. You can earn a little more interest with certificates of deposit (CDs) that lock in your money for a while (you choose the term to match your time frame) or low-risk investments like high-quality bonds or stocks (but be aware that those holdings could lose value). For your long-term goals, you can sit back and let your money work for you. With plenty of compounding time on your side, you could end up with more money even though you're putting away less. Here, you can go with riskier choices, like stock-based ETFs that have the potential for a lot of growth over time.

THREE MAIN STEPS FOR YOUR BUDGET

Budget, Revise, Repeat

Making a budget is not a one-shot deal: it's an interactive, evolving, flexible plan that requires some ongoing attention. You'll experience many life changes, from getting raises to moving houses. As you go through these events, your budget will come along with you. And even when you're not going through a change in your life, your budget may need to.

After all, your finances aren't static. Even fixed income and expenses can change. For example, new tax laws can change your take-home pay even if your salary stays the same. Other items that get deducted from your paycheck (such as health insurance premiums) could increase, resulting in less take-home pay. On the expense side, even steady expenses like your rent or mortgage payment can increase periodically. And inflation almost always hits expenses harder than income, meaning your regular monthly costs will go up faster than your salary.

First, though, you have to build your initial budget based on the information you have now, your current income and expenses. Then, as your financial situation changes or you decide to manage your money differently, you'll make appropriate changes to your budget.

BUILD YOUR BUDGET

To create a workable budget, no matter what platform you decide to use (pen and paper, software, apps), you need to gather some information and analyze it. Luckily, there are some very quick and easy ways to do it that don't involve you poring over receipts and doing a bunch of math (although if that's what you prefer, you can work out your budget on paper).

The idea is that you need to know—not guess—how much money you have coming in, how much you're spending, and what you're spending it on (most people are very surprised when they realize where their money is actually going).

Income and Spending

On the income side, you'll include all the money you can count on receiving. That includes things like your paycheck, business income, interest and dividends, child support and alimony, and cash from any other reliable sources.

The spending side is a little more complicated since money usually flows out to more places than it flows in from. Start with your fixed expenses, the ones that are the same every month, such as your rent or mortgage payment, minimum credit card payments, loan payments, insurance, cell phone bill, and savings. Tackling variable expenses is a little trickier, so you'll have to look at a few months' worth to get a good sense. These would include things like:

- Electric bill
- Groceries
- Gas
- Clothes
- Socializing

Inside the fixed and variable categories, take a look at which expenses are necessities and which are discretionary (things you don't need to get by).

Once you have all of that information in front of you, you can start making decisions about what you want to be doing with your money. Your budget will set the framework for those choices, laying out how you want to split up your income and where you want to make spending changes.

Food Plummets, Housing Soars

The way Americans divvy up their budgets has changed dramatically over the past few generations. The Bureau of Labor Statistics looked back over 100 years of family budgeting and came up with some very surprising findings. In 1900, families dedicated 43 percent of their budgets to food and just 23 percent to housing. Flash forward to 2003, and those staples flip-flopped, with families spending 33 percent of their income on housing but just 13 percent on food.

FOLLOW YOUR BUDGET

Once you've created your budget, you have to follow it to see if it works for you. Try to stick with the spending limits you've set, even if it's tough, in order to see if you've created a realistic budget that you can actually live with.

In order to follow your budget you'll need to do some planning or it will be very hard to stay on track. For example, now that you have assigned a specific dollar amount to spend on groceries every month, plan your meals and create shopping lists that stick to the budget rather than just walking around the store and grabbing what looks good. When a budget category runs out of money, stop spending money in that category for the rest of the month.

One of the easiest ways to help yourself stay on budget is to automate as much of your spending as you can. Setting up automatic bill payments makes sure everything gets paid every month, on time, protecting you from expensive late payment fees. Automate your savings so the money you've designated for goals doesn't get used for discretionary spending instead.

Equally important is to stop spending with your credit cards until you get the hang of following your new money plan. Credit cards make it much too easy to go over budget, which will make your next month's available cash even tighter.

Using budgeting apps can help you stick to your budget in a way that some other budgeting methods (which we'll talk about in Chapter 4) can't. Because they track your cash in real time, you'll be alerted when you're coming close to topping out an expense category.

REVISE YOUR BUDGET

As you work to stick to your budget, you may realize that some of the numbers just don't work or eventually stop working. That calls for a budget tweak to make sure your money plans fit your real life and your true spending patterns. Just make sure that your total budgeted expenses don't exceed your income and that you're not budgeting to accommodate overspending.

When you're working with a budget for the first time, several of your estimates may be off. That's especially true if you decide to include some spending cuts, and they go too far. For example, if you budgeted $400 a month for groceries and you actually spent $600 on food, that line item needs another look. Also, if you notice you're frequently stealing from "groceries" to pay for "clothing," you'll need to either adjust the dollar amounts assigned to your budget categories or keep a closer eye on your spending.

You'll also revise your budget whenever there's a change in your life or financial situation. Events such as getting a raise, having a baby, or selling a house will dramatically change your cash flow situation. Making sure your money plan reflects the "new normal" will help you keep your financial goals on track.

TRACK AND MEASURE YOUR SUCCESS

Hit Those Checkpoints!

Once you've set SMART goals and created a budget that will help you meet them, you'll be able to easily track and measure your financial progress. Periodically monitoring that progress lets you see in an instant whether the goals you've set truly mesh with your current budget. If they don't (and they probably won't for many budget beginners), use what you've learned to make your goals more achievable.

In addition to making sure you're on track to meet your goals, check in on important financial benchmarks (like net worth, which you'll learn about in Chapter 2) periodically. Assessing your overall financial health can alert you to problem areas before they get out of hand.

WHEN TO CHECK IN

Checking your progress too frequently can be discouraging, sort of like weighing yourself every day and not seeing any movement. That can lead to budget-busting habits that knock your goals off track. At the same time, you don't want to go too long without measuring your progress because you want to catch and respond to setbacks as quickly as possible.

You're better off planning on monthly progress reports in the beginning and stretching that to quarterly check-ins once your finances are under control. For longer-term goals, like retirement savings, check in at least once a year to make sure you're on track and that your portfolio still syncs up with your investment strategy.

Try a Goal-Tracking App

Monitor your success in a goal-tracking app like Strides. This app lets you enter your SMART goals (they have helpful templates) and measure your progress with colorful charts (green when you're on track, red when you're not) and stats to keep you motivated. You can learn more at www.stridesapp.com.

HOW TO MEASURE YOUR PROGRESS

When you set your SMART goals, you also created a concrete way to measure your progress. For each goal, figure out where you are in the time frame. For example, if you gave yourself eight months to meet a goal, and it's now two months in, 25 percent of the time frame has elapsed.

Then multiply the total dollar amount of each goal by the percentage you just calculated. For example, if your goal was to save $800 in eight months, to be on track you'd need to have 25 percent of that, $200, saved by the end of month two.

Now measure your actual progress against the goal you set. If you've saved at least $200 toward that goal, you're on track to reach it within the assigned time frame. If you're not quite there, look back to see where the disconnect happened and whether it was some kind of glitch (like you entered the wrong amount into the automatic savings transfer) or a budget issue (you had to pull from this savings to cover other expenses).

To fix a glitch, correct it and rework your budget to make up for the lost time. Fixing a budget issue calls for resetting your goal to match with the amount you really can afford to put toward it, at least for now. The easiest way to do that is to stretch out your time frame. For example, if you budgeted to save $100 but can only reasonably save $70, calculate a new time frame based on the $70 savings target (instead of using the time frame to come up with the target savings amount).

HOW TO PERFORM A FINANCIAL CHECKUP

In addition to tracking your budgetary goals, monitor these four numbers periodically to keep an eye on your overall financial health.

1. Net worth (the amount of money you'd have if you sold everything and paid off all your debt)

2. Debt-to-income ratio, or DTI (your total debt divided by your annual income)

3. Credit score (a number assigned to you by a credit rating agency that indicates your likeliness to pay back debt)

4. Credit utilization ratio (the percentage of your total available credit that you're using right now)

Follow these key financial measures to make sure they're moving in the right direction. You want your net worth and credit score to be increasing, and your DTI and credit utilization ratio to decrease or remain steady. While there's no target value for net worth, you can look at the average for your age range (according to the US Census) to see how yours measures up. For your credit score, aim for 750 or higher. For abundant financial health try to keep both your DTI and credit utilization ratio under 30 percent.

KEEP YOUR BUDGET FLEXIBLE

Yoga for Money

Your life isn't the same every day or every month, and your income and expenses won't be either. Some kinds of income, such as birthday cash and tax refunds, are more unpredictable than a regular paycheck. Some expenses (such as groceries) normally fluctuate, and others (such as tax bills) crop up only once in a while. Plus, there will just be times when you spend more than you planned to.

When you build your budget with wiggle room, you won't have to start from scratch every time your actual numbers don't match your plans. That wiggle room comes from spending less than your income and putting as much money as you can into savings. When you need or want something that's not in your regular budget you'll have the cash on hand to fund it.

Flexibility also comes in handy for people who cringe at the thought of detailed spending categories. In those cases, strict spending rules can lead to budget rebellion. To avoid that budget meltdown, you can build flexibility into your everyday budget, making it easier for you to stick to. The downside: It's tougher to track your spending, so you may not see potential budget busters that are keeping you from meeting your goals. Still, it's better to follow a loose, flexible budget than none at all.

ADD IN A FLEX-SPENDING CATEGORY

If you don't want to feel pinned down by rigid spending categories, you can create your budget with a catchall flexible spending category. To do that, you need to have other top-level categories to make sure your crucial costs and SMART goals get covered first. After that, spend the rest as you will.

Here's how to set this up. Make a list of the expenses that absolutely must be covered every month: housing, cell phone, loan payments, minimum credit card payments, and child care, for example. Make sure you include all the bills you have to pay, and don't forget the ones that pop up only once in a while (like renewing your driver's license or getting an oil change). The costs in this category take the first piece of your income.

Next, list the monthly contribution for each of your SMART goals. The total here gets the second slice of your income pie.

The Seven Most Common Unexpected Expenses

What kind of expenses will take you by surprise? Here are the seven most common:

1. Emergency room visit
2. Broken-down car
3. Emergency pet care
4. Last-minute travel
5. Cracked tooth
6. Burst pipe
7. Job loss

Once your necessities and goals are covered, all the rest of your income goes into that flex-spending category. This covers all of your day-to-day spending, from your breakfast burrito to new wireless earbuds—whatever you decide to buy. It's still a good idea to know what you're spending money on, but you don't have to go into superdetailed tracking as long as you're not overspending here.

PLAN FOR THE UNEXPECTED

Unexpected costs can crop up at any time, and it's important to be as prepared as possible for surprise expenses. Though you can't predict when these high-cost emergencies will happen, you can put a financial readiness plan in place for when they do. That plan will protect you from turning to budget-busting debt when you're hit with an unexpected expense.

A healthy emergency fund is your first line of defense for keeping these unpredictable costs from devastating your budget. When you have enough available cash to pay for an occasional emergency expense, you won't have to rely on credit cards or other borrowing to cover these bills, making them even more costly.

The second part of this financial defense: having enough and the right kinds of insurance to protect against those emergencies that might hit. Make sure there's room in your budget for crucial insurance premiums so your coverage doesn't lapse when you need it most. Health insurance, for example, helps shield your finances against catastrophic medical expenses. Homeowners or renters insurance covers both your living space and your personal belongings. Auto insurance takes care of fixing or replacing your car after an accident. And while virtually all insurance policies include deductibles (the amount you have to pay before insurance kicks in), they often pick up the lion's share of costs in the face of an emergency.

LEAVE SPACE FOR SLIPUPS

There will be times when you blow your budget—it happens to virtually everyone. The trick is to accept the slipup and move on. If you want to make sure that occasional slipups don't blow your whole plan or make you want to ditch budgeting altogether, set up a separate savings pool that can cover the excess.

Sometimes slipups are just expenses you forgot to account for, like haircuts and holiday shopping. After you've been on a budget for a full year, you'll come across all of the expenses that you inadvertently overlooked. You can either add in line items to catch these occasional costs or make a better estimate for the "extras" savings pool you created.

If slipups happen frequently, you'll need to rework your budget because it doesn't reflect the way you're really using your money. For example, say your plan allows $200 for entertainment and eating out but you consistently blow past that. Instead of throwing out your whole budget or just ignoring it, find a way to increase the allotment for that category, either by reducing a different expense or covering it with extra income.

Chapter 2

Know Where Your Finances Stand

Taking a deep dive into your finances can seem scary, especially if they aren't in good shape. Don't let that fear keep you from taking this critical step. You can't move your finances forward—get out of debt, build wealth—without a fixed starting point. Even if your finances are in terrible shape, or worse than you realized, you can fix them. Once you know your true financial picture, not just what you think is going on, you can figure out what to do next.

Every aspect of your finances matters here, not just the big stuff that most people focus on, like debt. You'll take a look at your take-home pay, your spending habits, and your retirement savings. When you look at the things that feed your financial situation all at once, the path to prosperity will become clear, and you'll be better able to make choices that drive your finances to the next level.

TAKE AN HONEST LOOK AT YOUR SITUATION

Put Everything on the Table

You've decided to take charge of your finances, and creating a budget is a key part of that. Before you can decide how you're going to spend your money, though, you need to take a thorough and wholly honest look at your current financial situation. No matter what that is, there's room to improve your financial standing, and your budget can be framed to do just that.

The truth is that most people don't know as much as they could about their finances. For example, you know you have a retirement account but may not regularly check the balance or the holdings (how the retirement money is invested). Or you may not know how much interest you're paying every year on your debt (and the amount will probably shock you).

Getting all the information and seeing it in front of you will clarify your true current financial position and offer important insights into how to make it better. Armed with that knowledge, you'll be able to set clearer priorities and goals, and it will be much easier to monitor your progress toward meeting them.

IT'S JUST WHERE YOU ARE

No matter what your financial situation is right now, it's your starting point. It doesn't matter whether your finances are in pretty good shape but you need help moving them forward, or you're drowning in debt and having trouble making ends meet. Either way, the most important thing you're going to do is the next thing.

That doesn't mean you shouldn't look backward at all. Understanding how your finances got to this point is an important part of moving forward. Judgment, fear, anger, blame, and guilt are not, but they're easy emotional traps to fall into, and they can sabotage your intentions. Accept your situation, acknowledge the behaviors that brought you to this point, and get ready to make a plan to take control of your money.

WHAT YOU NEED TO KNOW

Your full financial picture is made up of more than paychecks, bills, and loan payments, though all of those play key roles in your money situation. Most of us tend to look at only small pieces of the picture, focusing mainly on the familiar parts. Looking at the big picture every once in a while opens up a new perspective. That will give you a better read of your overall financial health and provide important clues toward the best next moves.

Here's what you need to know to see the big picture, your full financial situation:

- Net worth
- Monthly income and expenses
- Cash flow
- Credit score
- Complete debt details, including balances, interest rates, and expected payoff dates
- Complete retirement account information, including balances, contribution amount and percentage, asset allocation, and average returns

• Financial goals details, including current progress

Don't worry if you aren't sure what some of those are; we'll talk about them in more detail later. The important takeaway here is that your finances are more than the amount of money you have left (or come up short) at the end of the month. You need all of the information in front of you to make your best financial plan—and that includes a budget that suits your life and your current money situation.

JOINT FINANCES

If you and your spouse or significant other are working together to create a family budget, you'll both need to look at what you're each bringing to the table. Even if the two of you don't have any combined accounts (not even one), your finances will still be closely connected.

This can lead to an uncomfortable conversation, especially if you don't normally discuss your finances (and most people don't). Creating a joint money plan calls for full disclosure of all things financial and an honest discussion of your joint and separate priorities. This clear, no-holds-barred communication is the only way to avoid the kinds of money issues that can tear couples apart.

Having an honest money talk is not a one-time thing. To keep your finances on track, it's important to meet about money regularly (at least once every few months), go over your budget, and talk about upcoming changes.

Here are some ways to make sure this conversation happens regularly:

• Make a date for your money talk and have it in a café or coffee shop where you both feel comfortable (being away from home helps prevent distractions)

- Exchange written financial "reports" on the big-ticket items, such as retirement savings, debt, money goals, and money mindset to get the conversation going
- Listen to each other without interruption or judgment to keep the discussion flowing—virtually everyone has made financial mistakes, and most of us are afraid or embarrassed to talk about them
- Come up with joint goals and plan ways to reach them together

The more often you have these open discussions, the easier they'll get. If your conversations seem to devolve into arguments, consider calling in a third party like a financial advisor or counselor (sort of like a money therapist) to help the two of you communicate more effectively.

The Salary Secret

According to a 2018 survey by Aspiration (a financial services company), 48 percent of men and 40 percent of women don't tell their significant other how much money they earn.

ASSESS YOUR ASSETS
You've Got This

Assets are the things that you own, from the cash in your checking account to the clothes you're wearing to the MP3s on your phone. Some of your assets could be sold for cash. Others might not be sellable but would cost money to replace. Assets can be physical things or intangible (like those MP3s), living things (like pets), things you own on paper (like mutual fund shares), and even something you own but don't actually have yet (like custom furniture that's being built).

What Doesn't Count?

Just because you have or use something doesn't mean it's your asset. For example, if you rent a furnished apartment, you don't own the furniture. If you've borrowed it or leased it, don't include it as one of your assets.

This is where your financial picture first starts to take shape, by taking stock of everything that's yours. Once you know what you have and what it's worth, you can start to accumulate assets more strategically. That means minimizing assets that decline (depreciate) in value, and building up assets that increase (appreciate) in value or add to your income, a solid way to increase your personal fortune.

TAKING INVENTORY

As you begin to piece together your full financial picture, the easiest place to start is with what you have. So the first job on your assessment list is to take an inventory of your assets and assign each one a dollar value. This inventory will include mainly big-ticket items, then a big catchall category to capture all of the small stuff.

Here are some of the usual assets that people have: • House

- Car (and other vehicles)
- Retirement savings
- Non-retirement savings
- Investments
- Business
- High-value personal belongings (jewelry, artwork, furniture, major appliances, musical instruments, collectibles, etc.) The catchall category includes your stuff, lower-value belongings that are tough to stick a price tag on. This category can include things such as dishes, silverware, books, small appliances, and sports equipment. You don't have to do a detailed listing of your stuff, only a rough estimate of anything that could realistically be sold on eBay or in a yard sale.

How to Value Major Assets

Some asset values are simple and straightforward: your savings account has a definite balance, for example. Other asset values, such as your house or your car, can be a little harder to pin down and may take a little detective work on your part. Here's how to figure out realistic values for all of your main assets: • **House:** You can find the approximate fair market value of your house on websites like www.zillow.com or www.redfin.com. You can also ask a local realtor for comps (comparable home sales) in your neighborhood to get a clear picture of what your home could sell for.

- **Car:** You can find an approximate resale value for your car online at Kelley Blue Book (www.kbb.com) or Autotrader (www.autotrader.com). You'll need to know your mileage and enter realistic information about your car's condition for a reliable estimate.

- **Retirement savings:** Look up account values on the most recent statements for your 401(k) account (or other employer-based plan) plus any IRAs (Roth and traditional) or self-employed retirement plan savings.

- **Non-retirement savings:** Add up the current balance of your savings accounts, checking accounts, money market accounts, and CDs based on the most recent bank statements.

- **Investments:** If you have a brokerage account (at Vanguard or E-Trade, for example), pull the current value of your holdings from your most recent account statement. If you hold individual stocks, find their current market price; you can find that information easily online on sites like Yahoo! Finance (https://finance.yahoo.com). If you have individual bonds, the issuer's website usually has current market values. You can find out the current value of US savings bonds by entering some basic information about them on the US Treasury website at www.treasurydirect.gov.

- **High-value personal belongings:** The best way to value these is with a professional appraisal. If you don't want to shell out the cash for that, start with any receipts you have for a baseline value or check with your insurer (they often keep track of values for insured items). You may be able to find estimates for some items online at websites like www.invaluable.com. For things like major appliances and furniture, you can look on sites like www.craigslist.org or https://offerup.com to get a good idea of how much money you could get if you sold them.

Don't get too hung up on finding exact dollar amounts for assets other than savings and retirement accounts. Go with the most reasonable estimates you can find, and move on. You're doing this to give yourself a better idea of what you have, and close enough is good enough.

Don't Forget These Often-Overlooked Assets

There are a few assets people tend to forget about, but they still count toward your net worth. Some of the most commonly overlooked assets include: • The cash value of life insurance policies

• Money that other people owe you (including tax refunds you haven't received yet) • Prepaid cemetery plots

• Prepaid gym, golf, or country club memberships • Credit card rewards points and travel miles

If you have any of these assets, add them into your inventory to come up with the most accurate total asset value.

LIST YOUR LIABILITIES

Know What You Owe

Your liabilities are your debts, the money you owe to someone else. This part of your financial picture is easier, though less pleasant, to account for, but the information is essential to your future plans. Almost all liabilities come with a price tag—interest—that eats into the money you have available to live your life.

Debts can cost you more than money: they can keep you from taking advantage of opportunities that can benefit your finances. They can trap you in negative financial whirlpools that are hard to escape. Liabilities can hold you back, and they keep you from achieving your financial goals and building wealth. The first step toward defeating debt is to face it.

THE DETAILS OF YOUR DEBTS

Your next step in the budgeting process is to list all of your liabilities, from your mortgage to your credit card balances to that old bill from the dentist that you never quite got around to paying. Include every debt, even ones that you are not currently paying (like student loans), to see what they're doing to your finances. This liability list will include five columns:

1. Name of the creditor
2. Current total loan balance
3. Interest rate
4. Minimum monthly payment
5. Expected payoff date

If there's any additional information you have about a particular loan (for example, a variable interest rate, or an introductory 0 percent interest rate), include that on your list as well.

Americans in Debt

In April 2018 (according to the Federal Reserve), Americans owed an overwhelming $3.89 trillion! Included in that alarming figure is $1.52 trillion of student loan debt and $1.03 trillion in credit card debt. What's more, all of those numbers were around 3 percent higher than just a month earlier.

Once you've listed everything, total up both the "current total loan balance" and "minimum monthly payment" columns to create a full picture of your liability responsibilities. Both of those numbers give you crucial information about your overall financial picture. While it's important to know the total amount of money you owe, your total minimum monthly payment has a direct impact on your everyday life and your budget.

Secured versus Unsecured Debt

There are two main types of debt: secured and unsecured. Secured debt is attached to an asset; for example, a mortgage goes with a house, and an auto loan goes with a car. Unsecured debt, like credit card debt or personal loans, doesn't have a specific asset backing it up.

Because secured debt is tied to an asset that the lender can repossess (if you stop making payments), it usually comes with lower interest rates and better loan terms than unsecured debt. Some experts consider this "good" debt, but all debt comes with interest, and every dollar you pay in interest is a dollar that doesn't go toward building your wealth.

Unsecured debt, on the other hand, normally comes with higher interest rates, sometimes so high that it's nearly impossible to pay down the balance. Because there's nothing for the creditors to take back if the debt is unpaid, they'll typically enlist collection agencies or sue to get their money back. Other examples of debts that fall under the unsecured umbrella include student loans and medical bills.

Amortizing and Revolving

In addition to secured and unsecured, debt can be amortizing or revolving. Amortizing debt means that your loan balance is set the day you borrow the money and that every payment reduces your loan balance. You know how much your payment will be every month as well as the eventual loan payoff date.

Most amortizing loans come with fixed interest rates, but some come with adjustable rates. That means your interest rate may change periodically, which in turn changes your monthly payment. The terms are clearly spelled out in the loan agreement, so you can always predict when and how much your rate and payment will change. While these occasional payment changes will affect your monthly budget, they don't affect the final payoff date of the loan.

Revolving debt, which includes credit card debt and home equity lines of credit (or HELOCs), changes all the time. Like amortizing debt, your balance decreases when you make payments, but that's where the similarity ends. The big difference is that you can borrow more money without taking out a new loan. Every time you borrow more (like using your credit card to buy things), your loan balance increases. Because of these balance ups and downs, there's no specific loan payoff date; in theory, you could owe money on this type of debt forever. Plus, your payment is often based on your balance, so it can change from month to month, making it harder to plan for in your budget.

TOXIC DEBT

Ultra-high interest debt, also called toxic debt, is deadly to your finances. This undesirable debt category includes things like payday loans, personal loans, no-credit-check loans, and high-rate credit cards. The interest rates on toxic debt can be so high that you can end up paying two to three times more than you originally borrowed (and sometimes even more!), even if you make full payments on time every month. And even though you're making regular payments, your debt balance doesn't go down. If you are carrying this type of debt, make paying it off a high priority in your budget, or you could get locked in a damaging debt cycle (meaning you need to continually borrow more money just to stay afloat).

FIGURE OUT YOUR NET WORTH

Calculators Permitted

Your net worth is an important measure of your overall financial health, and it can help you track your progress toward accumulating wealth. Basically, your net worth is the amount of cash you'd have or owe today if you sold everything you owned and paid off all of your debt. There's no magic net worth number to aim for, but generally positive and growing is better than negative or shrinking.

The equation to help you calculate your net worth is simple: Assets – Liabilities = Net Worth. That's it—well, at least that's the math part of it. What it means to your overall financial picture depends more on how it changes than on where it stands.

Don't freak out if your net worth is negative, especially if you're under age forty. It's not unusual for younger people to have negative net worth because they're paying off student loan debt and haven't had a lot of time to start accumulating assets. The fact that it's negative doesn't matter. What does matter is where it goes from there. Along those lines, if you're retired, your net worth will probably start to decline. That's because after retirement, you move from an accumulation phase into a "using up your assets" phase, which naturally decreases your net worth.

Once you know your current net worth, you can measure your progress to see whether your wealth is increasing or decreasing. If your finances are getting off track and your net worth is dropping, you'll know to look into where and why so you can take the right steps moving forward.

How Does Your Net Worth Stack Up?

If you want to know how your net worth measures up, look to the median (not the average) for your age range (as reported by the United States Census Bureau). Here's how median net worth falls out by age:

AGE BRACKET	MEDIAN NET WORTH
Under 35	$6,676
35–44	$35,000
45–54	$84,542
55–64	$143,964
65–69	$194,226
70–74	$181,078
75 and older	$155,714

Remember, this includes everyone in the US, from struggling students to billionaires, and people in every state (state statistics vary widely).

SMART MONEY MOVES PUMP UP YOUR NET WORTH

Good financial choices, like saving for retirement and paying down your mortgage, build up your net worth. Any time you increase your assets or decrease your liabilities, you increase your net worth at the same time. And when you consistently spend less than your income, you're making the smartest money move of all.

Other smart moves you can make to boost your net worth include: • Investing in growth and income stocks • Investing in rental real estate

• Paying off debt (especially toxic debt)
• Increasing your savings

• Building a business

These actions have a cumulative effect, and as you make additional smart money moves, you'll see bigger, faster changes in your net worth. For example, paying off your debt has a double benefit of getting a liability off your books and ending outgoing interest payments, freeing up more money to snap up appreciating assets. In turn, those assets increase in value and increase your income, adding another double bonus to your net worth.

BAD MONEY HABITS UNDERMINE NET WORTH

Overspending is an obvious bad money habit that can take a toll on your financial well-being, but it's not the only way to tank your financial health. In fact, some bad money habits may seem like good money habits, and those can be much harder to spot.

• "Saving" on sale items if you didn't need them • Earning points on your credit card by buying more than you need • Snagging free delivery by adding more items to your shopping cart • Cutting expenses by canceling or not getting necessary insurance • Putting all of your savings into risk-free accounts instead of investing All of those habits chip away at your net worth, some more directly than others (such as those cloaked bad spending habits). Not having the right kinds and amount of insurance won't affect you until disaster strikes, like a tree branch landing on your car or your basement flooding, but then the lack of coverage can decimate your finances. While keeping your money somewhere safe seems like a smart plan, the ultra-low interest you'll earn in savings accounts can't keep pace with inflation—and that means your money will actually lose purchasing power over time, something that prudent investing helps you avoid.

Very bad money moves include things like high-risk investing, day trading, and cosigning for someone who can't get a loan on his or her own. Those moves have the potential to put your net worth in jeopardy, so protect your financial future by steering clear.

Using Credit Cards Can Deflate Your Net Worth

It's hard to believe that paying for your lunch with a credit card can have an impact on your net worth, but anything (even something small) that increases your debt has that effect. In fact, the biggest threat to your net worth is high-interest debt, and that includes credit card debt.

When Using Credit Cards Makes Sense

There are people who use credit cards to their advantage, and they do it by following three simple guidelines. Only charge what you can afford to pay for immediately. Never exceed 30 percent of your credit limit. And earn rewards toward things you would normally buy.

Consider this: You have a credit card that charges around 17 percent interest, and you buy a $2,000 sofa. If you don't buy anything else with that card and make an on-time minimum payment of $80 every month, it will take you almost eight years to pay for your sofa and cost you a total of $3,160 (including interest). That means you paid more than $1,000 extra for that sofa, and your net worth dropped by $1,160! Now multiply that idea by three or four credit cards, ongoing purchases, and growing balances to see how damaging this debt is to your financial health.

KNOW YOUR CASH FLOW

Where Does All the Money Go?

The way money moves in and out of your household impacts your financial health. Managing that cash flow the right way is one of the key secrets of getting ahead, and handling it the wrong way can lock you in a dangerous financial cycle. And if your cash flow is unpredictable, it's even more important to nail down the movement patterns.

Timing can make or break your budget. If the money you have coming in doesn't sync up with the bills you have to pay, you could end up in a budget desert, where you don't have enough cash on hand to cover your expenses even though you're bringing in enough income on paper.

When you know your cash flow situation, you can avoid those temporary budget deserts and make sure your checking account doesn't get overdrawn simply because of bad timing.

PAY ATTENTION TO TIMING

Even a predictable income can leave you short if your money-receiving and bill-paying schedules don't match up: you can't pay a bill on the tenth of the month with a paycheck you won't get until the fifteenth. That situation is even tougher for people living paycheck to paycheck, who don't have bridge savings to cover that timing gap. It can also be tricky for small business owners and freelancers who don't have predictable income.

There are a few things you can do to deal with this:

• Ask your employer to shift your paycheck schedule.

- Give customers incentives to pay you quickly.
- Reschedule some or all of your bill payments.
- Build up a bridge savings account.

The quickest, easiest of these is rescheduling bill payments. Many creditors (from credit card companies to utilities) will let you choose a pay date and change it online. You'll have less control over money coming in than money going out, so tackle that first.

Next, figure out how much you can expect to be short based on which bills are often paid late. Start to build a bridge savings fund (keep this completely separate from your emergency fund) to cover any lingering gaps. That can feel impossible if you're living paycheck to paycheck, but it can be done—it will just take a little longer. Start with microsavings apps like Qapital or Tip Yourself that let you save very small amounts, and watch those tiny savings turn into a thriving bridge fund over time. Keep replenishing that fund until you can better synchronize your cash inflow and outflow.

THE DEPOSIT MATERIAL MATTERS

How money flows into your checking account matters almost as much as when. Knowing more about how your bank processes different kinds of deposits and payments can keep you from getting zapped by an unfortunate time lag.

When you're putting money into your account, banks seem like they're acting in slow motion. That's because they can place "deposit holds," delaying access to money you've put in. Some deposits show up the next business day, others on the second business day. When that clock starts may also depend on the time of day you make the deposit. As long as you get the deposit in by 2:00 p.m. (banks can make the cutoff later than that but not earlier), it counts as being deposited that day; if you miss the cutoff, it will take an extra day for your funds to be available.

Depositing cash or receiving direct deposits gives you the quickest access, while depositing physical checks can delay your cash receipt by days.

In some cases, deposits can take much longer—even a whole week—to become available in your account. Here are the most common reasons for these extra-long delays:

- Your account is new
- You've been overdrawn several times before
- You deposit more than $5,000 at once
- You make your deposit at a "foreign" ATM, meaning one that isn't part of your bank's network
- You're redepositing a check that originally bounced

When you know how long it will take for the money to actually appear in your account, you know to wait before trying to use it. Account for that deposit lag in your budget to make sure you don't come up short when you're paying the bills.

FIX CASH FLOW PROBLEMS

If you're having a hard time managing your personal cash flow, and you're running out of available money even though your income is greater than your expenses, there are practical things you can do to increase the stream. Some will give you access to more cash right away; others will take a few months to kick in. But all of them will help improve your cash flow situation.

- Reduce your withholding taxes to get more take-home pay (but be aware this could end up in you owing money at tax time).

- Create a cash cushion account to cover any gaps in cash flow.
- Sign up for "personal financial assistant" Trim (www.asktrim.com) to free up cash by canceling forgotten subscriptions and negotiating lower cable and Internet fees, as well as setting up cash flow alerts (like minimum balance warnings).
- Add extra income streams for steadier cash inflow (see Chapter 5 for ideas).

Using any of these strategies will help you free up some money every month. Controlling your cash flow before a problem pops up is the best way to avoid expensive overdraft fees and late payment charges.

How to Change Your Withholding Taxes

You can reshape your paycheck by changing your withholding allowances. Use the withholding calculator on the Internal Revenue Service (IRS) website (www.irs.gov) to figure out how many allowances to take to increase your take-home pay. Then fill out a new W-4 form for your employer and wait for your instant "raise" to kick in.

TALLY YOUR INCOME

Rake It Up

When you're figuring out how much money you have to work with, look at all of the money you receive regularly, no matter the source. Even if it doesn't count as income for tax purposes (like child support), it still counts as income on your budget because it's money coming in.

Your budget will be based mainly on the income you can rely on: you know exactly how much you're receiving and when it will come. So if, for example, your sister owes you $2,500 and she's promised to pay you $100 a month, don't include that money as income in your budget unless she's already started making payments. If you budget up to expected income rather than actual income, you could end up in a budget hole where you run out of money before all of your expenses are covered.

NET NOT GROSS

When you're adding up your income, you'll need to know whether the money you receive is after-tax or pre-tax, meaning whether income taxes have been withheld. To budget accurately, you'll include only after-tax income, also called net pay.

It's easy to figure out the net pay from your job: it's the amount of your paycheck that's left after taxes, retirement plan contributions, and other deductions are subtracted from your gross pay. But income from other sources probably will be a gross amount, so you'll have to do a little math to take out the related tax bite, transforming it into net.

If you earn freelance income, for example, there won't be any income or other taxes (like Social Security and Medicare) taken out of the checks you receive, but you'll still have to pay all the regular payroll taxes. When you get a check from a client, you have to withhold taxes for yourself (30 percent to 50 percent, depending on your tax bracket and your state income tax situation) for budgeting purposes, basically giving yourself take-home pay to work with.

The same idea works on taxable (non-retirement) investment income. If you're earning a lot of money on your investments, you'll need to account for taxes so you don't budget that money for something else. Unlike earned income (which only includes money you worked to bring in), you won't pay any Social Security or Medicare taxes on that money. Instead, the type and amount of tax you'll pay depends on things like the type of investment income you receive and how long you've held on to the underlying investment. Here's a quick overview of how this breaks out:

- Interest gets taxed at your regular income tax rate unless the source is a municipal or state bond (those are almost always exempt from federal—and often state—income tax).
- Stock dividends (which can come from individual stocks, mutual funds, or ETFs) get taxed based on how long you've had the investment: if it's sixty days or less, they're taxed at your regular rate; if it's more than sixty days, they're taxed at a special lower rate based on your income level.
- Capital gains (money you earn when you sell an investment for a profit) get taxed based on how long you held the investment: if it was one year or less, you get taxed at your regular rate; if it was more than one year, you pay a special, lower long-term capital gains tax rate.

If you have a lot of non-retirement investment income, especially if it's coming in from a lot of different sources, you may want to work with an experienced tax accountant to help you figure out how much tax you'll owe so you can budget for it effectively.

Should You Make Estimated Tax Payments?

If your non-job income (income without taxes taken out) will leave you with a year-end tax bill of $1,000 or more, you need to make quarterly estimated tax payments to the IRS. Skip those, and you could be on the hook for penalties and interest. You can learn more about estimated tax payments at www.irs.gov.

ACCOUNT FOR OCCASIONAL INCOME

You may have some irregular but predictable (or at least easy-to-estimate) sources of income that you can include here, the same way you'll include occasional expenses in your budget. For example, if you have an annual garage sale that usually brings in $400 to $500, you can include the lower end of that into your total budget income.

Other examples of occasional income may include:

- Birthday or holiday money
- Tax refunds
- Insurance reimbursements

Don't include occasional income that's more like a one-time thing, such as a prize or a special performance bonus, in your budget. Instead, treat that like found money and put it toward your highest-priority goal.

Dealing with Unpredictable Income

Some people don't have steady, predictable income, and that can make budgeting a little trickier. If your paycheck fluctuates wildly (due to things like changing hours, overtime, or commissions) or most of your income comes from running your own business (which includes freelancing), base your budget on the least amount you can realistically count on bringing home in one month.

Look back at your monthly income over the past two or three years (or as long as you've been freelancing if it's less than that). Pinpoint your lowest income month and set that as your standard expected budget income. Then tally up your monthly expenses and figure out whether you can cover all of them with your standard income number. If you come up short, prioritize your expenses in order of necessity until you run out of income. As long as all of your needs are covered, this will be your backbone budget—a budget that fits your income.

Because you've budgeted based on your lowest income, you'll likely have money left over most of the time. Decide what you would like to do with that "extra" money. Smart choices include:

- Creating a safety net account (different than your emergency fund) to fill in any income gaps if you have a month that brings in less than the standard
- Making extra debt payments, which will eventually reduce your expenses
- Adding it to your retirement savings
- Putting it toward one of your financial goals

Remember to use a portion of your extra money (at least once in a while) to treat yourself—a night out, new boots, a weekend away, whatever makes you happy—as long as you have enough of a cash cushion to cover your expenses if your income drops.

TRACK YOUR SPENDING

Be a Budget Bloodhound

To build a reasonable budget, you need to take a look back at your normal spending patterns—and get ready to be surprised. This is really about your everyday spending more than your bills, but sometimes even regular monthly payments can surprise you. The real shockers usually come from casual and credit card spending. You know you buy lunch every day, for example, but you may not realize that's costing you more than $200 a month. Tracking your expenses is the only way to know how much cash you're shelling out every month, and you need that information to make a realistic budget.

Once you have a good idea of your normal spending, you'll incorporate it into your budget. If your income covers all of your expenses and lets you work toward your financial goals, you may decide to leave spending as it is. But if your budget comes up short, look for ways to cut back on any overspending you've discovered. Your budget will include target expenses, the amount you plan to spend.

To make sure you're sticking to your plan, you'll need to track your spending going forward, preferably in real time. The easiest way to do that is with an automated budgeting app, but there are other ways to do it if that's more comfortable for you (we'll talk more about this in Chapter 4). Regardless of your method, successful budgeting calls for tracking so you know how much you're spending.

FIVE BENEFITS OF TRACKING

The point of tracking your spending is to empower your decision-making with accurate information. If you want to spend $500 on takeout every month and you can afford it, do that. But if the realization that you're spending $500 a month on takeout makes you feel queasy, you can choose to cap that spending at $100 and funnel the rest toward your student loan payments (or another financial goal you've set).

Tracking gives you the opportunity to make conscious, informed choices about where your money is going. It transforms accidental spending into a choice that you control. That's why tracking is crucial for creating and sticking to your budget and beginning to build wealth. And, yes, it can be a pain to pay attention to everything you spend all the time (especially in the beginning), but doing it offers up some very desirable benefits.

1. **Sharpen financial awareness.** When you see where your money is going, you can make conscious spending choices.
2. **Uncover spending issues.** Small spending leaks can go unnoticed when you don't track spending; finding them helps you plug them before they drain too much money.
3. **Prevent budget overflow.** Tracking your spending works as an early alert system to make sure you don't overspend in any budget categories.
4. **Motivate cutback behaviors.** Knowing how much you're spending can inspire money-saving habits (like turning lights off when you leave a room or strictly sticking to a grocery list).
5. **Clear the wealth path.** Every dollar you spend is a dollar that's not working for you, and mindful spending sets the foundation for building wealth.

The biggest benefit of tracking is to connect you directly with your finances. That builds financial know-how and confidence, two qualities that can speed that path to wealth.

DON'T FORGET OCCASIONAL EXPENSES

Going back over a year's worth of bills and payments can help you capture things like trips to the dentist, haircuts, and holidays, but it may not pick up more intermittent expenses. These are costs you will definitely incur at some point—it's just a matter of timing. Setting up a spot in your budget to cover these occasional expenses can prevent you from raiding your emergency fund or turning to credit cards when they crop up.

What kinds of expenses fall into this bucket? Generally, it's for bigger items that will need to be replaced or undergo major repairs within the next three to ten years. That could include things like:

- Mattress
- Laptop
- Water heater
- Carpet
- Bicycle
- Car

You can get out ahead of these potentially budget-busting expenses by pre-saving for them. Then, instead of needing to finance them and pay a ton of interest, you'll be ready when they strike.

HOW DO I KEEP TRACK OF EVERYTHING?!

The idea of tracking your spending is probably overwhelming, but it's actually easier than it sounds, and you'll get used to it pretty quickly. There are so many different ways to pay, but all of them except for using cash are already recorded automatically. Every payment you make by debit card, credit card, PayPal, apps, check, or bank transfer leaves an electronic (or paper) trail that you can easily trace. Limit the way you pay (use only one credit card, for example), and you'll have fewer methods to track.

Simplify to Save Time and Money

You can cut back on tracking time by simplifying your spending. Fewer shopping trips mean fewer transactions to track, and when you plan ahead, you'll be more likely to reduce spending. An added budget bonus: less time in stores means less exposure to impulse purchases.

When you're first starting out, look over your electronic spending records every day and pull them together (in a notebook or a spreadsheet, for example) to see where your spending stands. If you do go with a budgeting app, it will automatically pull in all of your electronic spending in real time to give you a current overview.

All that's left to track are your cash purchases, so write them down in a notebook or hold on to your receipts any time you pay with money. If you tend to be a cash spender, you can also try the opposite approach here and use the envelope budgeting method (more detail on that in Chapter 4). To do that, you pre-assign your cash to specific expenses, each with its own envelope, to help you track your cash.

Chapter 3
How to Create a Livable Budget

There's no point in creating a budget you can't live with. That's why your budget has to reflect your needs, your finances, and your plans. There are dozens of different ways to budget and thousands of financial gurus bombarding you with advice. Go with whatever feels right for you and ignore everything else.

Your first budget won't be perfect. It may not even work. If that happens, don't give up on making a plan for your money; just scrap that budget and make a different one. It may take a little time to get this right, and when you do, you'll get a rush that comes from being in control of your money instead of worrying how you'll get through the month.

THE BASIC BUDGET EQUATION

Income and Expenses

No matter what type you choose, all budgets start in the same place with a very simple equation. Two main numbers will figure into your budget: income (the money coming in) and expenses (the money going out).

In its most basic sense the budget equation starts with income and subtracts expenses. If the result is positive, you have a surplus. If the result is negative, you have a shortfall. If the result is zero, you've successfully accounted for every dollar. No matter which result you get, creating a better plan for your money will bring you closer to your goals more quickly.

As straightforward as that two-part equation is, there are a lot of different ways to solve it. Pick whichever method feels the most comfortable for you. If you decide you don't like it for any reason (too much math, not enough detail, etc.), try a different method or create your own formula. Whichever approach you can stick with is the format that will work for you.

The Track Everything Budget

When you hear "budget," this traditional method is probably what comes to mind: tracking every expense individually to see how each measures up to your preset spending targets. This approach works well for detail-oriented people and people who really want to get a handle on their spending. It's also a good choice for budget newbies, because tracking everything is the only way to see where money is really going.

Luckily, software and apps can do all of the time-consuming tracking tasks so you won't have to devote too much time to your budget after you have everything set up. Once you've gotten a good handle on your finances, you can switch over to a more big-picture method if tracking everything becomes burdensome or unnecessary.

Where Did It Go?

Spending habits vary widely by generation, according to a 2016 report by the US Department of Labor. Millennials spent the most on motorcycles and musical instruments, but the least on ice cream. Gen Xers spent the most on almost everything, from alcohol to cleaning supplies to shoes. Baby boomers spent the most on pets, jewelry, and healthcare, but the least on furniture.

The 50–30–20 Budget

If you're comfortable with big spending buckets, the 50–30–20 budget plan might work well for you. Instead of drilling down to line-item expenses, this method takes a big-picture approach where all cash outflow gets sorted into three categories:

1. 50 percent to needs
2. 30 percent to wants
3. 20 percent to savings

The trick to using this budget is carefully separating out needs and wants. For example, apples and Pop-Tarts are both groceries, but Pop-Tarts wouldn't count as a "need."

What about debt? Minimum debt payments fall under the needs category, while extra debt payments get lumped in with savings.

The 80–20 Budget

Sometimes called the "pay yourself first" plan, the 80–20 budget separates savings from everything else. Every time you get paid, the first 20 percent goes straight into savings and the rest goes into one big spending pile. That doesn't mean all 20 percent has to go into a single savings vehicle; split it among your retirement savings, emergency fund, goal-based savings accounts, and extra debt payments. As with the other big-picture budgets, you can adjust the percentages to better suit your savings style.

The Zero-Sum Budget

With the zero-sum budget, money in equals money out every month. That doesn't mean you'll have no money in the bank at the end of the month, but it means you won't have any money left in your budget. That's because in this method, every dollar gets assigned to something: needs, wants, savings, or debt payment, for example.

To get started with this, you follow the traditional budget idea of writing down your monthly income and expenses (which include savings). The goal is for income and expenses to be equal—but it usually doesn't work out exactly that way the first time around. So if you bring in $4,000 a month, $4,000 will go out. If you happen to have any money left over at the end, you give it a job so you can get back to zero.

The "Debt Diet" Budget

Oprah's "Debt Diet," created with advice from financial experts, uses a five-category approach to budgeting. It's more detailed than just the simple 50–30–20 but not as cumbersome as tracking everything. Spending in each category is based on a percentage of your take-home pay. Remember, these percentages and categories are guidelines, and you can adjust them if they don't quite fit your life.

The five categories include:

1. Housing: 35 percent. This includes everything to do with your home, from the rent or mortgage payment to utilities, insurance, and repairs.
2. Transportation: 15 percent. Any expense related to your main means of transportation goes here, including things like car payments, gas, parking, oil changes, and public transportation costs.
3. Other living expenses: 25 percent. This catchall category covers everything else you spend money on, including things like food, clothing, vacations, concert tickets, electronics, and pet care.
4. Savings: 10 percent. If this seems low for covering retirement, emergency funds, and goals saving, remember that it comes from take-home pay, so any employer-based retirement contributions have already been made.
5. Debt paydown: 15 percent. This category covers student loan, credit card debt, personal loan, and extra principal payments toward your mortgage and car loan (the regular monthly payments were accounted for in the first two categories).

If you have another big, regular expense (such as child care or ongoing medical costs), add in a sixth category. Pull the funding for that from housing, transportation, and other expenses rather than from savings or debt paydown.

TWO WAYS TO BALANCE

Increase Income or Cut Expenses

When it comes to balancing your budget, you have two choices: cut expenses or increase income. Most old-fashioned budgeting books and financial experts go straight for expense cutting, advising you to do things like make your own coffee and get rid of Netflix, but that's a much more difficult way to go. It's often easier to increase income than cut expenses, creating more room in your budget for the things you want to spend your money on.

The best budgets do a little of each: increase income and cut out unintentional or unnecessary spending (things you don't even realize you're spending money—or too much money—on). When you take that double-sided approach, you'll be less likely to feel deprived and more likely to make quick financial progress that moves you closer to your goals.

BUMP UP INCOME FOR MORE FINANCIAL FREEDOM

Bringing in more money is a great way to free up space in your budget, especially if you've been living paycheck to paycheck. You'll probably have more control over this side of the equation, which makes it less frustrating to focus on than digging around for more places to cut back. Plus, that extra income cushion can help you avoid late and missed payments, which can save you money in fees and penalties, automatically lowering your expenses.

Whether you find a way to increase your income at your current job, find a lucrative side gig, start using apps that pay cash, or some combination of income-boosting strategies, you'll make more headway toward your goals. If you're looking for a permanent boost, start developing income streams, investments of time or money that you set up today to provide income later. The more of these income streams you create, the less work you'll have to do to keep the income flowing. (You'll find dozens of ways to increase your income in Chapter 5.)

What You Could Do with an Extra $100

As little as $100 goes further than you think. If you earn an extra $100 a month, you could build a $1,000 emergency fund in less than a year, make extra student loan payments and save thousands of dollars in interest, or invest it and let it bring in even more money for you.

TRIM EXPENSES WHERE YOU CAN

The number one rule of budgeting (of financial health, really) is spending less than your income. Even if you're already doing that, you may still be overspending, and that can keep you from reaching your financial goals and building wealth. Review your spending for a few months and look for expenses that are higher than you expected or that you didn't even realize you were paying. If you notice overspending—meaning spending more money than you intended or could afford—in any budget category, that's your starting point for cutbacks.

That doesn't mean you need to pinch every penny, buy only no-brand groceries, and stop having fun. Rather, it calls for putting a stop to any spending that doesn't serve your goals and cutting any expenses that don't add value to your life. Every dollar you don't spend on something you don't really need (or even want) can now be used toward what you would rather have, whether that's a house in five years or more money for going out with your friends this weekend.

LIVE WITH THE SURPLUS, NOT ON IT

Virtually everyone spends up to his or her income, and when that income increases he or she bumps up spending, a phenomenon called lifestyle creep. There's nothing wrong with that as long as you're aware of it, all of your financial goals are being met, you're not taking on more debt, and you're not constantly worried about money. If you're making a decision to boost your lifestyle, rather than just falling into it, you'll retool your budget to make sure spending doesn't spiral out of control.

But just imagine what your finances would look like if you didn't do that—or at least didn't let your spending creep all the way up.

Consider this: You get a hefty raise, and instead of buying a better car or moving into a nicer apartment, you don't. Instead, you use that surplus to supercharge your debt paydown or stash it in savings and investments. Now instead of spending more just because you can, you're making the conscious choice to build personal wealth.

SAVING IS YOUR NUMBER ONE EXPENSE

The Path to Wealth

Financial comfort starts with savings. Once you have some money put aside, and you aren't desperately waiting for your next paycheck to pay bills, a whole new financial world will open up to you. You'll have more freedom and more choices, and those will only grow along with your savings.

This is the true path to wealth: holding on to your money instead of spending it. That's why your highest-priority expense is stashing money in some form of savings account. It doesn't matter if you save $10 or $200 at a time; what matters is getting into the habit of keeping some of your money for yourself. Once you start a savings habit, you'll be amazed at how fast your money accumulates, and that may inspire you to put even more money away.

TAP INTO THE POWER OF COMPOUNDING

When it comes to building a sizeable nest egg, you need as much time on your side as possible. The more time you have, the bigger your savings will grow—even if you stop adding to the account—thanks to a powerful wealth-growing trick known as compounding.

Here's how compounding works. You put $100 into a savings account, and it earns $2 in interest (that's a 2 percent interest rate). Now you have $102, which earns $2.04 in interest, bumping your new account balance up to $104.04, even though you haven't added any more money to your savings. (You'll find the highest interest rates for savings accounts through credit unions or online banks.)

With the magic of compounding, you can let your money do all the work for you. Over time, your money starts to grow faster and faster because you're earning interest on a higher balance all the time.

That's the secret key to building wealth: time. When it comes to your savings goals, more time means more money. There is no second chance to capture the power of compounding. Time makes all the difference, so use all of the time you have and start saving right now.

SAVINGS PRIORITY 1: GET YOUR FREE MONEY

If you have a 401(k) plan through work and your employer offers a match, take it. That means contributing enough of your own money to get the maximum match amount. If you don't, you are leaving free money on the table.

An employer match is extra money that your employer contributes to your retirement account based on the amount you contribute. For example, your employer could offer to match up to 3 percent of your salary in 401(k) contributions. If you earn $50,000, your employer would contribute a maximum of $1,500 (3 percent of $50,000). To get the full $1,500 match, you would have to contribute $1,500 of your money into the account. If you only contributed $500, the match would be $500, and you'd be losing out on $1,000 of free money.

SAVINGS PRIORITY 2: TAKE ADVANTAGE OF COMPOUNDING

Your retirement account contributions don't need to stop at the match. You can contribute up to the legal maximum, supercharging your future nest egg. Not only will your contributions lower your current tax bill—unless you contribute to a Roth IRA or Roth 401(k) account—but the earnings will grow tax-deferred. That means you won't pay a penny in taxes until you start taking the money out, which helps your money grow faster through compounding.

The more money you stash in retirement accounts early on, the bigger your nest egg will grow—even if you contribute less overall than someone who started ten years later. You can't go back in time to take advantage of compounding, so put away as much as you can as soon as you can to let your money grow as much as it can.

SAVINGS PRIORITY 3: EMERGENCY FUND

Your car breaks down. Your dog chews up your smartphone. You lose your job. Unexpected expenses or income shortfalls crop up, and paying for them can put a serious crimp in your budget unless you're prepared with some emergency funds to cover them. People with even modest emergency savings take on less debt and have more financial flexibility than people with no emergency fund, giving them an edge when it comes to building wealth.

How big a safety net do you need in your emergency fund? Three months of living expenses (necessities) will give you enough breathing room to handle most emergencies while you work to get your finances back on track. To make sure you don't dip into this fund for regular expenses, keep it in an interest-bearing savings account that is not linked to your regular checking account. In fact, keeping it in a different bank adds an extra step to using that money, helping ensure you won't touch it unless you really need to.

That's Not an Emergency

Periodic or large expected expenses (such as a property tax bill or scheduled car maintenance) are not emergencies, so don't pull from your emergency fund to cover them. You know these costs are coming and at least approximately when, so you can plan to put money aside to cover them. Leave your emergency fund for things that are truly unexpected.

SAVINGS PRIORITY 4: SAVINGS GOALS

When you set your SMART goals, some of them were probably linked to savings. Each goal you set came with a dollar amount and a time frame, making it easy to figure out how much you'd need to contribute every month to stay on track. For example, if a two-week tour of Scottish castles costs $3,500 and you want to get there in two years, you'd need to save $146 a month.

After you've figured that out for all of your goals, add them up to figure out how much you'd need to save each month in total. Chances are, you won't be able to meet all of your goals by their deadlines (especially because they come after retirement and emergency savings on the priority scale). Even if you intend to start saving for only your top-ranked goals, they still may call for more funding than you have available. That calls for a little goal editing, which usually involves extended timelines. Maybe you won't be able to replace your car in five years without taking on debt and get to Scotland in two years, but moving the trip out another year or two makes both goals possible.

Now that you know how much you'll devote to each goal, you need a place to house that savings. To meet multiple goals, it's helpful to have a different space for each—but dealing with several savings accounts can be a big savings turn-off. Many online banks offer the option of "sub-savings," which lets you allocate your money among different goals all inside a single bank account. SmartyPig (an online savings bank, www.smartypig.com), for example, lets you set up different savings goals, complete with target balances and end dates. Every transfer into the primary savings account gets split up according to the goals you've set, and they automatically stop when any goal has been reached.

KEEP YOURSELF FROM DIPPING IN

One of the biggest barriers to savings is withdrawals. If you tend to dip into your savings for any reason other than their purpose (for example, tapping into emergency savings to pay for a party you hosted with your credit card), you'll need to find ways to stop that negative financial habit. When sheer willpower isn't doing the trick, try these tricks to safeguard your savings:

- Name your savings. Put a label on every savings account you have (emergency, house down payment, fun money, whatever it's for). That makes you less likely to withdraw the money for any other reason.
- Lock it up. Put the money for longer-term savings goals into time-locked CDs. You'll earn a little more interest and have less (but not no) access to that cash until the CD comes due.
- Hide it from yourself. Set up automatic deposits into the account, and include those in a different budget category. Don't connect the account to any apps or other bank accounts, and you just might forget you have it.
- Nix the debit card. If you don't have easy access to the cash, you won't be as quick to withdraw it. Set it up so you actually have to go into the bank to take out money.

Use whatever strategies you can to keep yourself from raiding savings, and you'll see your money stack up much more quickly.

SET YOUR SPENDING PRIORITIES

You Do You

Setting spending priorities is about figuring out what's most important to you.

Maybe you'd rather take a three-week beach vacation than buy a new car, or maybe the convenience of takeout every night tops a road trip to Coachella. Ranking your spending priorities helps make sure the things you really care about are covered in your budget and not crowded out by more mindless purchases. Spending priorities don't cover only big-ticket items; they factor into daily spending as well.

The key here is to spend your money on purpose. Pay attention to what you're buying, and take a second to consider the life cost (what else you could do with that money) as well as the financial cost. Then decide which is more important to you —and you've just set a spending priority.

SEPARATE NEEDS AND WANTS

It may feel like you need that latte every morning, but in the world of budgets, it counts as a want. Figuring out the difference between what you want and what you need is an important part of constructing a budget you can really live with. It's easy to confuse wants and needs, but when you break it down, needs include only the absolute essentials: food, clothing, shelter, medical care, child care, transportation for work (or school), and minimum payments on your debt. Everything else is a want.

To be clear, you need food to live; you don't need Thai takeout three times a week. You need clothes, but you don't need cashmere sweaters or twenty pairs of shoes. That Thai takeout and those cashmere sweaters are wants disguised as needs, and they can sneak through as high-priority budget items if you aren't careful. Make sure to label those types of purchases as wants so they don't bust your budget.

Don't worry: there's most definitely a place in your budget for wants. They just have a lower priority than the things that you really need to live.

THE PYRAMID OF NEEDS

When your budget is supertight and you're struggling to make ends meet, it's critical to prioritize your needs (wants are totally off the table here). If you can't meet all of your financial needs, some of your bills won't get paid, so you need to make sure the bills you do not skip are for things you could not get by without. Your priorities may be different here and there, but in most cases, this is the order to use for covering your bills:

1. **Housing.** Your number one priority is paying the rent or mortgage to keep a roof over your head.
2. **Utilities.** Having water, power, phone, and (for many people) Internet is priority number two.
3. **Other home-related expenses.** Any obligations related to your home, like property taxes and insurance, come next, especially if not paying them could result in losing your home.
4. **Things you need to get to work.** Anything connected to keeping your job or running your business—car payments, child care, gas—comes next in the list.

5. Minimum loan payments. Avoid expensive late fees, penalty interest rates, and other costs associated with default.

Any money that's left after these critical expenses are covered can go toward paying your other bills. (You may have noticed that food was not on this list; that's because the focus was on paying bills.)

UNDERSTAND OPPORTUNITY COSTS

Every time you buy something you don't need, you're sacrificing the chance to do something else with that money. Whatever you're giving up is the opportunity cost (or life cost) of that purchase. So while it may feel like you're sacrificing when you force yourself to pass up a splurge, it's really the opposite: when you splurge, you're sacrificing your goals.

For example, stopping at the local donut shop every morning on the way to work costs about $15 a week, or nearly $800 a year (if you pay cash, about $100 more if you pay with credit and don't pay your bill in full every month). Think about all the things you could do with $800—those are the opportunity costs.

When you feel the urge to buy anything that you don't need, whether it's a $3 cupcake or a $200 pair of shoes, think about the opportunities you're giving up. It'll take longer and cost more to pay down credit card debt. Your trip to Thailand will get pushed back another month (or six). If you still decide to spend the money now, that's okay because you've considered the opportunity cost and made a conscious choice about your purchase.

GO FOR THE GUARANTEED WIN

Every month, your money gets pulled in dozens of different directions that all feel important and that can leave your goals short. When that happens, it can be hard to figure out how to split up your goals money. Do you put less money in each? Do you put some on the back burner? The best way to figure out your solution is to prioritize your goals so you're prepared to handle occasional budget shortfalls.

One of the best strategies here is to go for guaranteed wins, putting money toward goals that reward you in concrete terms. For example, paying down debt is a guaranteed win because you absolutely save interest going forward. Beefing your retirement savings falls into this category, too, especially if your employer offers matching contributions—an instant guaranteed win. By choosing these guaranteed goal victories, you'll actually be able to meet your other goals more quickly.

SPEND LESS THAN YOU MAKE

Bring Back Some Change

It's the number one most important thing you can do to take control of your money and build lasting wealth, but it's also one of the hardest things for most people to do: spend less money than you make. There's constant pressure, both external and internal, to buy more, and it can be very hard to resist. In fact, the only way to thwart that pressure is to be aware of it and turn away.

Spending more money than you make does more than blow your budget. It puts your financial future at risk, forcing you to keep paying for the past instead of saving for the future. Overspending means that you are in debt, usually high-interest credit card debt, which shrinks your budget and traps you in a debt cycle. By putting an immediate stop to overspending, and committing to spending less than you earn, you're taking the most critical step toward getting your finances under control.

CREDIT CARDS ENABLE OVERSPENDING

You can't overspend money—actual money—because once you part with it, it's gone. Credit cards let you overspend without a thought.

Consider this scene: You bring $60 (your budgeted amount) to the grocery store. When the cashier rings you up, the total comes to $68. You have only $60 on you, so you have to put something back. But if the same situation happened when you were carrying a credit card, you'd just buy the extra stuff, whether it ran $8 or $38 over your grocery budget.

Debit Cards Do It Too

Debit cards also make it easier to overspend, but with a set stopping point. Once you've drained your bank account, you can't spend any more. But until that point, using your debit card can push you over budget and even lead to expensive overdraft fees.

Until you can stick to your budget even when you're carrying credit cards—meaning you'd still put things back until your total came down to $60 in our example—don't take credit cards with you when you go shopping.

TRY A SPENDING FREEZE

One way to knock down spending is with a temporary spending freeze. Here's how it works: for a preplanned period of time, usually no more than a month or two, you spend money only on absolute necessities. A move like this will bring your budget into sharp focus, which can help you weed out excess spending and jump-start progress toward your goals.

It can be hard to stick to a spending freeze, especially in the beginning, but it does get easier over time. In fact, many people who try a temporary freeze get so used to living without wants that they end up reducing their spending permanently.

What expenses would be allowable during a freeze? Just the bare necessities, including:

- Housing (rent or mortgage payments, gas, electric, and water, for example)
- Groceries (avoid prepared foods and snack foods)
- Transportation (to and from work or school, avoid unnecessary travel)
- Medical costs (such as prescriptions and doctor visits)

For your best chance of success, avoid shopping in real life and online. When you grocery shop, work from and stick to a list, and limit trips to the store to one per week.

A Family Freeze Challenge

If you have a couple's or family budget, you all have to agree to the spending freeze, or it won't work as well. To get other family members more excited (or at least less resistant) about these temporary extreme cutbacks, you can turn it into a contest, with a splurge prize for the winner once the freeze is lifted.

Your temporary sacrifices offer the perfect opportunity for an extreme budget reset. The freeze will clarify what you really need and what you can do without on your journey to more solid financial footing.

SET UP CONSCIOUS SPENDING RULES

If it's hard for you to pass up great deals and impulse buys, set up conscious spending rules to rein in those habits. These rules force you to think more about the money you're spending so you have to make a deliberate choice to make a purchase. Here are three examples of impulse-thwarting spending rules.

1. The "wait for it" rule. If you want to buy something that costs more than $100 (or $200 or $50, depending on your situation), wait a week before you do it. Use that wait time to figure out if you still want the something. If you do, look for a way that you can get it for less money.
2. The "indecision decision" rule. If you can't decide between two things you want to buy, don't get either. When you really want something, the choice will be clear.
3. The "something in, something out" rule. Any time you buy an item you don't need, something you already have (something comparable) has to be given away, donated, or

sold. If you're trying to downsize, make it a "two-out for one-in" rule.

Putting these types of rules in place will slow things down and get you used to thinking twice before you buy anything you don't need.

WORK PLANNED SPLURGES INTO YOUR BUDGET

When you deny everything you want, your brain will start to rebel and you'll be tempted to go on an all-out spree. To counteract that urge, build some room for occasional splurges into your budget. The best way to do this is with a special savings account that you can use sort of like a backward credit card: the balance will go up when you pay in and down when you pay out and earn interest in between. Don't put any restrictions on this account except a minimum balance that will keep it open.

Because you have to actively decide to pull money out of this account, you're more likely to use it purposefully, buying something you absolutely love or have been thinking about for a while rather than something that catches your eye in the moment that you may not still want tomorrow. When you figure out how you want to treat yourself before you start spending, you'll be sure to enjoy your splurge rather than regretting it the next day.

Geography Sets Prices

Where you live drives your costs for just about everything, from housing to gas to groceries. According to the Economic Policy Institute, the basic annual budget for a two-parent, two-child family in Brownsville, Texas, is $38,203, but in San Francisco it comes to $148,439. Before you make a move, think about how local costs will impact your budget.

SIDESTEP FINANCIAL QUICKSAND

Danger Ahead!

The quickest ways to tank your finances are overspending and using consumer credit (which includes credit cards and personal loans). Those two wealth-drainers usually go hand in hand, teaming up to trash your budget.

When you get stuck in the overspending/overusing debt cycle, you'll get caught in financial quicksand. Then you'll need to turn to debt for necessary spending because your minimum debt payments are taking up more and more of your budget, dragging you down into an increasingly deeper debt hole.

You can avoid that financially deadly trap, but success calls for a habit overhaul. You'll have to change your approach to money and budgeting and fight the overwhelming impulses to spend.

DON'T BUY INTO SOCIAL PRESSURES

The social pressure to spend money can be overpowering. You see other people's Instagram lives or coworkers driving up in shiny new cars, and it's natural to want the same—or better—things. You face constant pressure to upgrade your phone and other tech, post vacation pictures that your "friends" will envy, and sign your kids up for every activity available.

It's hard to ignore all of that social pressure, but falling for it will drain your budget and keep you from building wealth. The part you don't see on Facebook and Instagram is the growing mountain of debt or anxiety when bills pour in and there's just not enough money to pay them.

Next time you see one of your friends drive up in a new Lexus, look beyond the car to the payments that suck up a too-big chunk of his or her take-home pay. Look further and see the stress of needing to put the electric bill on a credit card because there's not enough left in the checking account to pay it. Remember that more expensive cars also come with more expensive parts, repairs, and maintenance that will chip away at his or her wealth. Don't buy into the social pressure of "keeping up with the Joneses" and focus instead on increasing your net worth.

DON'T LIVE UP TO YOUR INCOME

It's natural to go bigger as you start making more money: bigger house, better car, more exotic vacations. Even if you keep your expenses less than your income as you upsize (which most people don't do), they may not stay that way. Expenses go up almost always faster than income. When you've upsized, your expenses will automatically be bigger and will almost always increase faster.

On top of that, life changes add expenses. Buying a house costs more than renting, for example, and having kids increases costs by a lot more than most people expect (more on that in Chapter 7). Between these extra costs and rising prices, even high earners are struggling to make ends meet and often turn to credit cards to fill the gap—adding the extra expense of interest along with everything else.

There are a lot of ways that your expenses can change even if you don't buy more stuff, squeezing your budget to the limit. Leaving a decent-sized cushion between your income and your needs-based expenses acts like an inflation/extra-cost shock absorber. So, even when your income increases, think twice before you upsize your life.

BE CAUTIOUS WITH CREDIT CARDS

Using credit cards can trap you in a financial hole that seems impossible to dig out of. The more you use them, the more you'll need them to cover even basic necessities. Credit card companies love this and respond by raising your limit so you can spend even more. Before you know it, you owe thousands of dollars on your credit cards, and that balance will only grow larger even if you stop using your cards entirely.

Credit card (and other consumer credit, like personal and payday loans) interest is the biggest wealth drainer. The only way to keep it from drowning you in financial quicksand is to stop using consumer credit right away. (For tips on how to do that and pay off your consumer debt, see Chapter 6.)

DON'T FALL BEHIND BEFORE YOU GET STARTED

Student loan debt traps more people than ever before in negative financial territory. More than 44 million graduates owe around $1.48 trillion in student loans, according to Student Loan Hero (2018). The average college senior graduates owing $39,400 in student loan debt alone. That translates to a budget-busting average $351 monthly payment as soon as you're done with school, whether or not your first job pays enough to cover that along with your other living expenses.

Now add credit card debt on top of that. Credit card companies absolutely love college students and actively court them on campus with promises of building a credit history and coupons for free stuff, like food at local restaurants (the companies are not allowed to give out tangible gifts like T-shirts anymore while they're on campus). Around 56 percent of college students have and regularly use at least one credit card, according to a 2016 survey by Sallie Mae. Among that group, about 25 percent leave school with more than $5,000 in credit card debt.

Owing that much before you even get started on your financial future can be crippling. Make sure you fully understand the consequences of borrowing before you do it. Consider going to a less expensive school, taking some courses at a community college to reduce your overall costs, or getting a job to cover your living expenses so you don't end up with a pile of high-interest credit card debt on top of your student loans.

SAVINGS THWART FUTURE DEBT

Getting rid of the need to use credit cards prevents their drain on your finances. When you have savings to draw from, you won't have to rely on credit cards to pay your bills or make large purchases. Borrowing from yourself (a.k.a. making savings withdrawals) can save you thousands of dollars in interest, and paying yourself back is much better than gritting your teeth and sending money to the credit card company every month.

Plus, savings lead to money growth, whether you're earning 2 percent in a savings account or 8 percent in your retirement account. That's why savings is the main budget priority and the key to prosperity—not to mention a great way to easily skirt financial quicksand.

Millennials Are Superstar Savers

According to a survey by NerdWallet, millennials—especially millennial parents—are outsaving other generations by far. In fact, 38 percent contribute at least 15 percent of their income to retirement savings, compared to only 24 percent of Gen Xers and 23 percent of baby boomers.

AVOID THESE COMMON MISTAKES

Just Because Everybody Else Does It . . .

When it comes to personal finance, there are a lot of mistakes to make, especially when you're new to managing your own money. Basic financial literacy levels are alarmingly low. What makes that worse is that most people don't realize that they aren't financially literate, so they don't take any steps to improve their know-how, and they may not even realize when they make colossal money mistakes.

Recognizing, accepting, and learning from your financial mistakes will reshape your finances. You'll be able to fix your current money problems and avoid future setbacks when you know what to watch out for. This new awareness can help you get ahead and help make sure you never turn into a frightening financial statistic.

SKIPPING THE EMERGENCY FUND

Two-thirds of Americans wouldn't be able to come up with $1,000 in an emergency (according to Bankrate's 2018 Financial Security Index survey), and that includes families earning more than $100,000 a year. That means when expensive problems crop up, they're forced to turn to credit cards or other borrowing or risk losing crucial assets like a home or a car.

But having any amount saved in an emergency fund—even $250—can help you avoid complete financial devastation. Even small financial cushions can increase your financial security. So don't get bogged down in thinking you need $1,000 or more. Start small and build your emergency savings as fast as you can. If you have to tap into it for an emergency, refill it as soon as you possibly can so you'll be ready for the next one that inevitably occurs.

FORWARD SPENDING WITH CREDIT CARDS

Every time you use your credit card, you're borrowing money, even if you pay your balance in full every month. This habit of spending forward—buying now, paying later—puts you in a position to budget backward. Basically, you're spending money you don't have yet: next month's income. And because next month's income is already promised to pay the credit card, you can't use that income to cover next month's expenses, you're forced to put those expenses on the card, and you're trapped in a credit card cycle.

There are two ways to break out of this trap, and they both involve putting your credit card away and not using it, at least temporarily.

1. **Option one** is to slash your expenses to the bone and pay your credit card balance in full while paying cash for current expenses.
2. **Option two** is to pay cash for the regular expenses in your budget and not pay your credit card in full; rather, make whatever payment you can afford with the money left in this month's budget.

Once you've broken out of the forward spending cycle, you can start using your credit cards again as long as you don't overspend for the current month's budget.

NOT RETURNING STUFF YOU DON'T WANT

How many times have you kept something that was the wrong size or color, or that didn't work the way you expected, just because returning it would have been a hassle? Holding on to things that you bought but will never use is one of the most common financial mistakes (I've done it plenty of times) and also one of the easiest habits to break.

If you're feeling buyer's remorse, and there's still time to return the item(s) you purchased, return them. Most online shops make returns supersimple (and if they're not, stop shopping there), often providing prepaid shipping labels and posting instant cash back on the card you used once they get the package. If the e-tailer has a physical store, you can take your return there, a good choice especially if the company doesn't pay for return shipping. Return policies at physical stores vary widely, but most will take back any unused item with a receipt if you bring it back within thirty days. Whichever works with the stuff you want to return, take the steps to get it done.

This strategy works for things like gym memberships too. If you signed up for memberships, classes, or activities and you aren't going, cancel them. Be prepared to face a little sales pressure, but don't get persuaded to stick with something that you don't really want.

NOT PAYING BILLS ON TIME

Paying your bills late, even once in a while, can wreck your finances. In most cases, you'll be charged late fees, making next month's bills even bigger. These fees can range from just a few dollars to $100 or more, depending on the creditor. But where things really get sticky is when you're late with debt payments.

Paying credit card bills and other loans even one day late can trigger penalty interest rates that may be significantly higher than the regular rate. That means a larger portion of every payment you make will go toward interest, so less goes toward your loan balance, which keeps you in debt longer. Plus, all of that extra interest you're paying sucks up room in your budget, making it much harder to reach your financial goals or even make ends meet.

Reversing Your First

If you've always made payments on time before but somehow missed the due date for one, call the creditor. Remind the person that you've never been late, and ask him or her to remove any late charges and—even more important for your overall financial health—keep you at the regular interest rate instead of imposing the penalty rate. Most of the time, creditors will.

On top of all that, late payments show up on your credit report and lower your credit score. That means any time you want to borrow money in the future, it will be more expensive. You'll be charged higher interest rates on everything from car loans to mortgages. In addition, poor credit can make it much harder to get an apartment, a job, or life insurance.

MAKING MINIMUM PAYMENTS ON CREDIT CARDS

Around 30 percent of Americans make only minimum monthly payments on their credit card bills (according to the National Financial Capability Study), a huge money mistake. When you make only minimum payments, you'll be in debt years longer and pay thousands more in interest. If you're also using the credit card in question for purchases, you will never pay off that bill.

Making more than the minimum payment (even just $20 or $30 more) every month will knock time and interest off your debt—but only if you stop using the credit card. Doubling that minimum payment could cut your repayment period in half, so you'll be out of debt in two or three years instead of six. The sooner you start making bigger payments, the more you'll save in interest, keeping more of your money for yourself.

Chapter 4
Budget Mechanics

Once you figure out the money part of your budget, you'll turn to the logistics: the "how" side of budgeting. To come up with a system that suits you, you'll need to get in touch with your inner financial expert. Think about the ways you spend money, how you stay organized, and the way numbers make you feel. When you take all of those aspects into account, you'll get a sense of how involved you really want to be with your budget.

Then come the mechanics: how you'll enter, track, and analyze the information. There are several different ways to manage your budget, from a pen and notebook to fully linked-up apps. Which you choose depends on your comfort level with technology and privacy, an assessment of how hands-on you want to be, and an honest appraisal of how good you are at follow-up. No matter how this all shakes out, there's a perfect budget method for you, and this is how you'll find it.

FIND YOUR BUDGET PERSONALITY

Frugal or Frivolous?

Your budget will be as unique as you are, or it won't work for you. Now that you know where your finances stand and have set clear goals, you're ready to take all of that information and create your money plan. The type of plan you build will depend on your most pressing priorities and goals, along with your earning, saving, and spending patterns. Taking all of these factors into account will help you create a plan you can truly live with instead of a budget that leaves you feeling frustrated, a budget that you'll probably ditch before long.

YOUR MONEY PERSONALITY

Your budget really starts with you: the way you handle money now and whether you'd like to change your relationship with money. If you know your money personality, you can frame your budget accordingly.

- **Emotional spenders** buy more when they're angry, sad, or happy, and that can lead to impulse purchases and credit card debt that derails other budget goals. Creating spending blockades can help slow things down when the urge to shop strikes. Adding a special savings account to cover occasional overspending will help prevent excessive credit card debt.

- **Status spenders** live large, buying big-ticket items and keeping up with the latest everything. They're comfortable with risk (including risky investing) and debt, which can lead to budget breakdowns. By budgeting for those big purchases and occasional losses, they can smooth out financial ups and downs and avoid running up unmanageable debt.

- **Dodgers** avoid money stress by hiding from it (such as ignoring bills they can't pay). They don't think about or plan for the financial future so are often significantly behind on savings goals. Automating budget features (such as bill paying, expense tracking, and saving) reduces that stress and helps make sure nothing gets skipped.

- **Mega savers** tend to be future focused and risk averse, prioritizing financial security over everything else. They avoid debt and invest ultra-conservatively, but those choices can also take a financial toll in the forms of low credit score and savings that don't keep up with inflation. The budget can address this by adding back these riskier categories in a secure way.

No matter which money personality best fits your situation, your budget can bring better financial balance and reduce financial stress.

THE SIMPLE BUCKET BUDGET

For people who like to keep things supersimple, a bucket budget does the trick. This classic 50–30–20 budget keeps things at a big-picture level so you don't have to get bogged down in details. It's a perfect starter budget and one you can use as you're figuring out your financial priorities and goals.

Here's how it works:

- 50 percent of your income goes into the needs bucket
- 30 percent goes into the wants bucket
- 20 percent goes into the savings and investments bucket

Those percentages are not set in stone. For example, if your needs take up more than 50 percent of the money coming in, steal from your wants bucket (not your savings bucket). You can fiddle with the numbers until they make sense for your lifestyle.

THE DEBT-ERASER BUDGET

If your debt burden is crushing your finances, it's time to take charge. Setting debt paydown as your budget priority is the smart move here. This is where you'll see the biggest returns, more than even the most lucrative investments, especially if most of your debt comes from credit cards and other high-rate borrowing.

Medical Expenses Can Increase Debt

According to the National Financial Capability Study, 21 percent of Americans struggle with medical debt, and about 21 percent of those medical bills are past due. Overdue medical bills can hurt your credit score, and that can lead to higher interest rates on loans and credit cards.

With this strategy, any money that's not going toward necessities (which include retirement savings) will be used to pay down debt. You'll find specific debt paydown strategies in Chapter 6, which will help you figure out the most effective way to get rid of your debt burden and save tons of money in interest.

THE WEALTH-BUILDING BUDGET

This future-looking, no-more-worries budget focuses on creating and growing wealth. No matter how much money you have stashed away now, you can turn your budget into an amped-up savings plan. To achieve the overall goal here, you'll concentrate on adding income-producing assets to your net worth and minimizing spending on wants.

Once your needs are covered, your retirement and emergency savings are fully funded, and any debt payments are made, extra money in the budget goes toward buying assets. Income-producing assets include investments (such as stocks, bonds, and exchange-traded funds), rental real estate, and businesses. As these assets begin to produce income for you, you'll be able to increase your net worth even further.

THE ROOM-FOR-FUN BUDGET

If experiencing life is your top priority, you need plenty of room for fun in your budget—but that won't come at the expense of building up savings and paying down debt. This "here and now" budget carves out plenty of cash for the things you want to do: travel, scuba dive, host lavish dinner parties, whatever makes your life worth living. You'll still direct money toward savings (especially retirement savings) and debt payments, but any extra money in your budget goes into your "enjoy my life" fund.

To make this style work, you will have to make some trade-offs. You'll have less savings, and it will take longer (and cost more) to pay off your debt. Look for other places in your budget to slash costs, like downsizing your housing expenses or putting a hard freeze on buying stuff you don't absolutely need. You can also find ways to turn your experiences into cash, like selling photos taken on your rain forest trek or writing golf course reviews (you'll find more details about this in Chapter 5).

THE UNSTEADY INCOME BUDGET

If you rely on side gigs or freelance income, budgeting presents some extra challenges. It's harder to plan when you're not sure how much money you'll have coming in next month, so this budget focuses on necessary expenses first and follows up with income from there. The trick here is to create a minimum steady income—sort of like a paycheck to yourself—that covers all of your absolute needs (including savings and debt payments), then comes back around a second time to cover the rest (like extra debt payments, money toward savings goals, and fun money) with "surplus" income. It can take a few months for this budget to really kick in, but once it does you'll never worry about coming up short.

For this to work, you need to know your income highs and lows over the last couple of years. Look back over your records, and figure out both the least and most money you received in a month. (This is the money you actually got, not the amount you billed or expected.) For budgeting purposes, the lowest monthly income amount is the one to use when you're working to figure out those first-pass expenses. Since you'll probably bring in more than that most months, doing it this way builds in an automatic safety net. The "extra" money you bring in will go toward building a cash cushion.

When that cash cushion grows big enough to cover at least a full month's budget, you'll use it to create a steady "paycheck" for yourself, using previous income to cover this month's expenses. Whenever you get paid now, the money will go into the cushion account to be used for paying next month's bills. Any time you have a surplus, funnel the extra cash into your highest-priority financial goal.

GO LOW-TECH

Create a Worksheet

No matter where you decide to house your budget, you'll need to start with a collection of information. In order to create a budget that you can live with, you'll need to know how much money you have coming in and going out and where that money usually goes.

If you prefer to go low-tech, you can work out your budget with pen and paper. With data breaches being reported with alarming frequency and the prospect of ransomware locking up laptops, many people are going back to basics when it comes to budgeting. This method gives you the most control over how you split out expenses, always includes things in the right categories, and doesn't come with recommendations, alerts, or "advice" that may sometimes feel condescending. Best of all, you will be intimately familiar with your finances, and that's a great way to build financial confidence for a more prosperous future.

SET UP YOUR WORKSHEET

Whether you record your income and expenses in a notebook or throw receipts and check stubs in a shoebox, you need some way to put all of the information together every month to get a complete financial picture. Accounting ledger paper works well for this; it's what the expansive sheets were designed for in the first place. You can easily find ledger paper online or at an office supply store. It comes in a variety of sizes based on the number of columns you need, so pick the size that fits the number of categories you're tracking.

This classic accounting tool holds space for the details of every transaction: date, description, dollar amount, category, and any other information you want to track. If you want to track by month, you can organize each ledger sheet to hold an entire month's income and expense information by using different columns for different categories to sort your transactions. If you prefer to track by category, set up an individual sheet for each one, then one master sheet to put it all together. If you have the time, you can record every transaction as it occurs so you'll have constantly up-to-date data. Otherwise, sit down periodically (at least once a month) with your records and an extra-large latte (or a beer, a glass of wine, whatever makes you happy) and record them all at once.

Try Preprinted Forms

Most office supply stores have budget forms you can use to track your income and expenses manually. Some even come printed on expense envelopes, making it even easier to organize receipts and keep tabs on your spending.

Tracking is harder using this method, and that can make it difficult to see overspending until after the fact. If you want to go fully low-tech, you'll have to find a way (such as the envelope method) to stay on top of your daily spending to make sure you're staying within your budget limits.

DEALING WITH CREDIT CARD STATEMENTS

When you're working your budget manually, dealing with credit cards calls for double duty. In addition to tracking payments made for each card and its running balance, you'll need to make sure you've accounted for all of the individual charges in their proper budget categories.

Along with the regular expense-recording worksheet you set up, it's helpful to create a separate sheet for each active credit card, meaning any one card currently in use or with an outstanding balance. The individual card worksheets will contain only high-level information for each month, which you'll pull from the statement. Record these five data points, each in a separate column:

- Total new charges
- Total payments
- Interest charges
- Any fees (like for late payments)
- New statement balance

With that data all in one place (instead of spread out over a dozen credit card bills), you'll get a different perspective on your credit card situation. You'll notice different spending and payment patterns and see the direction your balance moves from month to month. These new insights will give you a bird's-eye view of your credit card usage and help you set better credit card–related SMART goals to get or keep debt under control.

THE ENVELOPE SYSTEM

This classic budgeting technique uses envelopes full of cash to help you monitor your monthly spending. It's a great way to get yourself used to budgeting: paying cash has a very different effect than swiping a credit card, and it makes you more aware of your spending. This helps you really connect with your budget because your finances seem more real.

On the hands-on side, you set up an envelope for each spending category in your budget: rent, groceries, utilities, clothing, gas, and so on. Then every pay period, you cash your paycheck and split the money up among the envelopes based on your budget categories.

If any of your envelopes has leftover cash at the end of the month, put most of that extra money toward your number one goal, and reward yourself for spending wisely with a (responsible) treat. If you run short of money, stop spending until your next pay period.

Some basic rules to follow:

- When an envelope is empty, spending for that category is done for the month. If you truly need more, you'll have to steal cash from another category and adjust your budget going forward.
- If you have to use a credit card to pay for something, immediately take the money out of the envelope for that category and move it into the credit card payment envelope.
- When you do combo shopping (like buying groceries and clothing at the same store), you'll pull money out of multiple envelopes to keep your categories correct.
- If you have an envelope that you never (or rarely) use, ditch that category and revise your budget.

You can also do a modified envelope system by paying your regular bills with checks and using the cash envelopes only for everyday spending. Figure out which works better for keeping you true to your budget, and go with that.

DIY SPREADSHEETS

Create an EXCELlent Budget

If you like working with numbers and details, a spreadsheet budget may work well for you. Spreadsheets offer a lot of flexibility because you're the one setting up everything, so you can tailor your budget to suit your particular needs. You choose the categories and level of detail you want to track. You can set up visuals (like pie charts) or big-picture budget summaries to get an idea of where your finances stand at a glance.

These budget platforms require basic spreadsheet know-how plus regular time and attention to stay up to date. Plan to devote time every week for data entry. If you're great at gauging your spending, you can stretch data entry to a monthly chore.

The potential downside: you won't have real-time data (unless you update your worksheet every time you make a transaction), so you won't know how well (or poorly) you're following the budget until after the fact. While that won't affect your regular bills, it can leave you in the dark about daily spending. To make sure you don't go too far down an overspending rabbit hole, update your everyday spending at least weekly, even if you update everything else monthly.

HOW TO BUILD A BUDGET SPREADSHEET

Creating your budget spreadsheet is pretty straightforward. You can set up your worksheet any way you like, as long as it includes these five main columns:

- Description (of income or expense)
- Category (paycheck, housing, food, insurance, etc.)
- Budgeted Amount (what you plan to spend or receive)
- Actual Amount (what you actually spend or receive)
- Over/Under (the difference between the budgeted and actual amounts)

Once those are set up, you'll list all of your regular expenses and their categories (for example, electric bill/housing category) row by row. Those first two columns (Description and Category) will be the same every month, sort of like your own worksheet template.

Next, type in the monthly amount you expect to spend for each expense or receive as income in the Budgeted Amount column. Enter income amounts as positive numbers and expense amounts as negative numbers. For fixed income and expenses, the numbers can be locked into your template so you don't have to enter them repeatedly. For income and expenses that vary from month to month, your budgeted amount will be your target—what you expect to receive and the limit on how much you plan to spend.

Built-In Templates

Spreadsheet software typically comes with built-in family budget templates. All you have to do is enter your information, and the template does all of the calculations for you. These are really helpful if you're a spreadsheet novice or just don't have the time to start from scratch.

To set up the Over/Under column, you'll enter a simple formula for each line: Actual Amount minus Budgeted Amount.

Enter sum formulas at the bottom of each of the money columns to see your budget totals. If the total for the Budgeted Amount column comes out less than zero, you'll need to reduce some expense targets or find a way to bring in extra income to balance your budget.

USE AN ONLINE TEMPLATE

There are dozens of free budget templates available online, and they're all pretty similar. You can download many of the prefab templates right into Microsoft Excel, then customize them to fit your needs.

Kiplinger (www.kiplinger.com) has a good beginner household budget form that's straightforward and easy to use. You choose the budget period, then enter your categories (they list dozens of expenses that you can customize) and your budget target amounts in the online form. Once you've tailored the template to suit your needs, you can download the worksheet and open it in Excel. This is good for setting up your budget, but it doesn't offer any preset tracking capabilities.

Vertex42 (www.vertex42.com) offers several different budget templates to choose from, and one is sure to fit your situation. You'll find worksheets for everyone from college students to families, covering a variety of time frames (weekly, monthly, and annually). Its Money Management Template is set up to track spending and create reports (complete with graphs) so you can get a good handle on your budget.

You can also find a good basic budget form in the Toolbox on the Consumer.gov website (www.consumer.gov), courtesy of the Federal Trade Commission.

If you want to keep your budget housed online so you can access it from anywhere, try one of the money planner templates in Google Docs. You'll find a few different options in the Google Drive Template Gallery (www.docs.google.com/spreadsheets).

HOW TO USE YOUR SPREADSHEET

At the end of every month (or week or day), you'll gather all of your financial documents, such as bank statements, credit card statements, pay stubs, cash spending logs, and receipts. Then you'll enter your income and spending line by line in the Actual Amount column. Once you've typed in those numbers, your spreadsheet will automatically figure out the Over/Under for each line item.

When you're all done, check out the total in the Actual Amount column to make sure it's zero or positive, and check the line and column totals in the Over/Under column to see how close you were to your expectations and whether you went over budget overall.

If your actual income and expenses matched up well with your projections, you can leave them as is. If some of your line items are too far off for comfort, look at the reason for the mismatch. A one-time difference (such as a high electric bill during a heat wave) doesn't require a budget adjustment, but an ongoing underestimate (or overestimate) calls for a budget rewrite.

SOFTWARE MAKES IT SIMPLE

Click, Click, Enter, Click, and Done

Budgeting software has been around for decades, and it's had plenty of time to work out all of the kinks. You'll spend a lot less time with setup than you would for a spreadsheet, but you may be more limited in your category and expense grouping options. Also, all of the budgeting software offers the option of linking your bank and credit card accounts so you can import information rather than having to type everything in yourself. Whether you prefer budgeting on your hard drive or in the cloud, there's a software solution for you.

THE BEST PROGRAMS FOR YOU

All of the budgeting programs included here also offer apps so you can stay connected to your budget all the time.

You Need a Budget (YNAB)

"Give every dollar a job" is the first rule in the YNAB method. This program works on a principle called zero-sum budgeting, where every single dollar gets accounted for, zeroing out your budget every month. YNAB is a subscription service that works through your computer to help you get control of your money. The program links with your bank and credit card accounts to import transactions and offers an app that will sync up with your computer so everything stays up to date. Focused solely on budgeting, YNAB doesn't bring in other aspects of personal financial planning like investment tracking.

You can try YNAB out for free for thirty-four days, and after that it costs $83.99 a year ($6.99 a month but you pay the full fee annually). You can learn more about this program at www.ynab.com.

Mvelopes

If you like the envelope method but not the idea of carrying all that cash around, look into Mvelopes. This software works the same basic way, offering digital envelopes for splitting up your money every month. It links to your bank and credit card accounts, lets you assign money to whatever envelopes you want, and lets you see what you've spent in the past. It also has an app that syncs up with your computer so you can manage your money on the go. Mvelopes has different subscription service levels, starting with the Basic version that costs $4 a month or $40 a year. You can take advantage of the thirty-day free trial at www.mvelopes.com to see if this budgeting method works for you.

Quicken

Quicken offers the soup-to-nuts version of personal finance software. The Quicken brand starts with a basic program and offers a ton of add-ons and upgrades as your needs get more sophisticated. Along with budget building, transaction importing, and expense tracking, you can use the basic Quicken software to do things like manage your bills and track your spending.

The bare-bones version is Quicken Starter, which costs $34.99 a year. Quicken Deluxe adds in debt tracking and investment monitoring services for $49.99 a year. Quicken Premier offers even more tools, like personal financial forecasting, portfolio management, and even tax advice, for $74.99 a year. Both the Deluxe and Premier versions offer the first year for a discounted price. All versions of Quicken have to be installed on your computer to get you started. Quicken also offers a free mobile app that will sync up with the software.

Find out which Quicken software might be right for you at www.quicken.com.

Family Ties

As of 2016 Quicken and TurboTax are no longer owned by the same company, but at tax time you can still easily transfer your Quicken data right into TurboTax to make creating your return easier and less stressful.

KEEP YOUR DATA SAFE

Whether you're using desktop or online software, it's critical to make sure your personal financial information is secure. These programs link to your bank and credit card accounts, and that means they have your passwords stored along with all the other sensitive information. Plus, software crashes and freezes can make your information inaccessible. So before you enter any information or set up links, take steps to protect your data.

- Make sure the data is encrypted and password protected
  - Run updated antivirus software on your computer
- Never use public Wi-Fi to update personal financial software
  - Back up your data regularly (especially if you're not using online software) • Use the most updated software version

As long as you're vigilant with these strategies, your personal financial information should remain secure.

BUDGET ON THE GO WITH APPS

I Gotta Know Right Now

If you want up-to-the-minute budget information 24/7 without the hassle of constant data input, budgeting apps will work best for you. Like software, these require a time investment for setup, including connecting your financial accounts and choosing your categories, but once that's done the app will do all of the updating for you. Every transaction from your linked accounts will be automatically pulled into your budget in real time, so there won't be any time lag when you're ready to check in—all you'll have to do is look at your phone and you'll know exactly where your monthly money stands.

Just the Apps

Both YNAB and Mvelopes offer app-only budget tracking if you don't want to deal with (or don't have) a computer, and the pricing is the same either way.

Budgeting apps usually also offer recommendations (like better deals on services you use), alerts (when you're nearing spending limits), and advice on how to manage your money (like when a credit card balance transfer might make sense). What's more, all of the budgeting apps listed here are free (or at least have free versions), so you don't need to worry about spending money to save money.

Mint

Tried-and-true Mint was one of the first budgeting apps, and it still ranks high on the popularity list. This app comes with a wide range of features to tie your whole financial life together, but the budget component is the centerpiece. Mint makes budgeting simple by pulling information from banks, brokerage firms, credit card companies, and other lenders so you'll have all of your information (from investment earnings to loan balances) in one place.

The app automatically tracks and categorizes your transactions in real time, so you can tell in an instant whether you're sticking to your budget. It offers up lists and colorful graphs so you can get the overview in a glance. You can even set up alerts to let you know if you are going over budget or running out of cash.

One downside: ads. For example, if you buy beach towels and sunscreen, Mint might serve you up an ad for sunglasses. If you hate having your screen cluttered up by these targeted ads, you might want to cross Mint off your list.

Wally Lite

If you want just a very basic budgeting app, check out Wally Lite. It keeps track of income and expenses as you go and serves up current budget snapshots to help keep you from going over. It even lets you take and save pictures of your receipts for your records, rather than having to enter expenses manually. It captures where you are (via location services) to automatically identify the type of purchase you're making for quicker categorizing, and the more you use it, the "smarter" it gets. The app also lets you set savings goals and track progress toward meeting them as part of your budget.

This app isn't as intuitive as some of the others and can be a little harder to navigate if you want to keep track of more than just your income and expenses. But if you mainly want to tap into its budgeting capabilities, it's very straightforward. On the downside, you can't access Wally through your computer, only through the app.

One unique special feature: Wally can handle foreign currencies (unlike most other budgeting apps), which can make a huge difference if you travel internationally or move out of the US.

PocketGuard

If you have trouble keeping your spending under control, the PocketGuard app may be able to help. Like other budgeting apps, PocketGuard links up with your accounts and compares your actual spending to your plan. You can set and track savings goals and set hard spending limits. It's also one of the easiest budgeting apps to set up, partly because it's budget-only focused and doesn't tie together your entire financial picture.

Along with its other features, PocketGuard actively looks for ways that you can save money on your regular bills (like phone or cable) by seeking out better deals. Plus, with its In My Pocket feature, you can see how much money you really have available to spend every day—not just the balance of your bank account. On the downside, PocketGuard doesn't track goals, like savings.

Simple

Simple takes a different approach by focusing on the banking side of budgeting. In fact, it essentially takes the place of a traditional checking account (complete with bill paying, a Visa debit card, and fee-free ATMs) with the added bonus of built-in budgeting. Anything you can do with a standard checking account, you can do here, like set up direct deposits, earn interest, and transfer money.

On the budgeting side, Simple tracks your spending and lets you set up envelope-like spending goals so you never go over budget. The app offers goal setting and tracking features, including a special spot for emergency savings. It also lets you know what's safe to spend based on what's really going on in your account (upcoming payments, for example) rather than just your available balance.

Goodbudget

If you're budgeting as part of a couple, the Goodbudget app can help. The Goodbudget system is based on the envelope method and lets you sync up two devices so you and your significant other will always be on the same financial page. This is a great way to track spending when you're not together so you can tell when an expense envelope is empty (or almost empty). The app also lets you split transactions among multiple envelopes, which works great when you're shopping in stores where one trip may hit several spending categories.

Keep It Private

If you're nervous about putting so much private financial information in one place, look at the app's security measures before you choose it. The best security includes high-level encryption, multifactor authentication, and the ability to shut down mobile access to your account if your phone goes missing.

The free version of this app offers ten envelopes and maintains one year of history. The Goodbudget Plus version offers unlimited envelopes and accounts, five-device connectivity, access to five years' worth of budget history, and email support for $6 per month (or $50 per year).

AUTOMATE SAVINGS AND PAYMENTS

Set It and Forget It

The real secret to successful budgeting (and wealth-building, by the way) is automation. Putting your money on autopilot makes your life easier and less stressful, and it sets you on a faster path to financial freedom. You won't have to worry about whether the bills got paid on time, and you won't forget to add money to your savings.

Plus, it's much harder to accidentally sabotage your financial progress when everything is automated. You won't rack up late payment fees or get hit with penalty interest rates on your credit cards, both of which can derail your financial plans.

LET YOUR EMPLOYER DO THE WORK

If your employer offers direct deposit and a retirement plan, you're two steps ahead in the game. Many employers will let you split your direct deposit between checking and savings, and that means you can direct part of every paycheck straight into savings without even thinking about it. Using the "pay yourself first" philosophy is the best way to supercharge your savings habit—especially when it takes a few steps to stop these automatic deposits. You can't just decide not to do it; it takes a payroll change. That roadblock means you have to give serious thought to canceling these savings transfers, making it much less likely that you will.

The same goes for retirement savings. When your employer deducts your contributions right from your paycheck, you'll barely notice that the money isn't there. This "forced" savings lets you make the choice to save once rather than having to make it every time you get paid. And as an added bonus, many employers will match at least a portion of your automatic retirement account contributions, so you get free money out of the deal.

SYSTEMATIC SAVINGS STARTS A HABIT

When an employer isn't doing the work for you, set up automated savings for yourself. Online banking makes it easy to create routine transfers into regular and retirement savings accounts.

You can also use a variety of apps to set up savings that sweep up little bits of change here and there. You'll barely notice these transfers as they happen, but their impact will be very noticeable when you've built up sizeable savings.

Be aware that some of these apps charge fees for their savings and investing services.

- Acorns uses a round-up approach to savings, gathering up the spare change from your daily debit and credit card transactions and investing it in your choice of stock portfolios. $1/month (free for college students for up to four years).
- Qapital is designed to help you automatically save toward specific goals based on the savings rules that you choose (or create). Free.
- Digit sneaks a little "extra" money out of your checking account every day based on your banking habits (it offers a no-overdraft guarantee) and puts it into a Digit savings account. Free for 100 days, then $2.99/month.

Some banks (such as Bank of America) offer round-up style and other microsavings options to their customers, so check in with your bank too.

PUT BILL PAYING ON AUTOPILOT

Online banking can be your budget's best friend, especially when it comes to paying bills. When you automate your bill paying, your bills will always be paid on time, letting you avoid the extra costs of late payment fees and penalty interest rates, not to mention dings to your credit score.

Reminders Prevent Overdrafts

If your income is stretched tight or varies from month to month, create checkin reminders in your online bank account. Doing that lets you make sure there's enough money in your account to cover all the automatic payments before they're made, so you don't end up overdrawing your account and getting hit with budget-busting bank fees.

There are basically two ways to set this up: through your bank account or through your creditors. Setting up automated bill payments through your checking account gives you more control, and it gives you the option of delaying, reducing, or canceling a payment if you realize there's not enough money to cover it. Setting up automated payments through creditors gives you less flexibility but may offer other benefits like reduced interest rates or other special discounts. Whichever way you decide to go, make sure your checking account is always fully funded with enough cash to cover your bills.

If you prefer to go the app route, look into Prism. This free app automatically keeps track of all of your bills (it collects data from more than eleven thousand billers in the US) in one place so you can see everything you owe and when payments are due at a glance. It also sends reminders so you don't have to worry about missing payments or paying late. Prism also takes care of paying the bills for you: you can set up automatic recurring payments, schedule bill paying ahead of time, or even send same-day payments—whatever works best for you.

Chapter 5

Easy Ways to Increase Income and Trim Expenses

Extra cash will free up your budget and speed up your goal timelines, whether you're racing to pay down debt or eager to retire early. There are two ways to increase your cash flow: boost income or trim expenses. Most of the time bringing in more money is easier than spending less because you have more control over income than expenses.

Even if you don't have time to add in a second job or a side gig, you can still bring in extra money every month without breaking a sweat. You can put your money to work for you, take advantage of cash-paying apps, even get a jump on creating future passive income streams that let you work once and collect cash for years. At the same time, you can try simple tricks to trim spending in ways you won't even notice. And tackling the problem from both sides at once will bring you the most reliable and sustainable results.

FOUR WAYS TO BOOST EARNINGS

Show Me the Money

Most budgeting advice focuses on cutting back by trimming expenses. That's why people associate budgets with deprivation, making it harder to stick with them. It also overlooks a huge part of the budgeting puzzle: income.

For many people, boosting income is easier than slashing expenses. The gig economy opens up a lot of opportunities, from driving for Lyft to renting out your spare room. More and more people are launching successful small businesses. The Internet makes it easier than ever to create passive income streams. And the quickest (and best) way to bring in more money without having to work more: squeeze more money out of your current job.

GET A RAISE

One of the best and most sustainable ways to increase your income is to get a raise. Since standard annual raises are usually based on a percentage of salary, you get a sort of compounding effect with every salary increase.

If it's been a while since you got a substantial raise, ask for one. The secrets to success here are preparation, practice, and patience: know your facts, rehearse your pitch, and give your boss time to think about a response.

Before you march into your boss's office to lobby for a bigger paycheck, make a list of all the reasons you deserve a reasonable raise (you can find appropriate salary ranges on websites like PayScale and Glassdoor). Focus on your skills and accomplishments, especially if you've been taking on additional or more complex tasks. Think about what sets you apart from other employees and makes your service unique. Let your boss know just how valuable you are and how much harder his or her job would be without you on the team.

Timing is also important here. You can increase your chances of a "yes" by:

- Formally scheduling time for the discussion
- Asking soon after a workplace victory
- Making the request ten to twelve weeks before your regular annual review

Most importantly, be prepared for the possibility that your boss might say "no." It's discouraging, but it's not necessarily the end of a longer-term conversation. If there's no room for a raise in the budget, you can try taking another approach and asking for something like professional development opportunities or some additional vacation time.

FIND A SIDE GIG

There are tons of ways to make extra cash, many without leaving your couch. Lots of side gigs come with flexible hours, so you can work whenever (and sometimes even wherever) you want.

With all of the opportunities available in the gig economy, you can easily find a side job that fits your skills and schedule in no time. For example, you can:

- **Take online surveys.** In under thirty minutes, you can earn cash or rewards points (redeemable at places like Amazon or iTunes) from online survey companies such as Swagbucks (www.swagbucks.com), Opinion Outpost (www.opinionoutpost.com), and VIP Voice (www.vipvoice.com), or with apps like i-Say by Ipsos.

- **Test websites.** Typical gigs last about twenty minutes, where you'll visit the target website, evaluate it, and report back to companies like UserTesting (www.usertesting.com), Userfeel (www.userfeel.com), and TryMyUI (www.trymyui.com).

- **Join an online jury.** Lawyers use mock juror panels to try out their cases, and you can get paid for your opinions. Mock jurors can find work through companies like OnlineVerdict (www.onlineverdict.com) and Resolution Research (https://resolutionresearch.com).

- **Be an online tutor.** Companies like Chegg (www.chegg.com) and VIPKID (https://t.vipkid.com.cn) hire tutors in a vast variety of topics and may even let you choose the age group (grade school, college, or adult) that you prefer to work with.

Your Side Gig Might Be a Business

Even if you don't think of your side gig as a small business, the IRS might. That means you can deduct work-related expenses from the money you earn, which lowers your taxable income and your tax bill. Keep track of receipts and mileage during the year, and remember to account for them at tax time.

There are also plenty of choices if you prefer to leave your house while you're earning money. You can drive for Lyft or Uber, do odd jobs for TaskRabbit, or go mystery shopping for BestMark or IntelliShop. Great sources for general freelance work are Upwork and Indeed. People with high-level professional skills and experience can bid on consulting projects through companies like Catalant and Expert360.

Keep in mind that there are a lot of scams floating around. The main thing to watch out for: if a company is charging you an upfront fee to start earning with them, find a different company to work with.

DEVELOP PASSIVE INCOME STREAMS

Passive income streams work in two basic ways: you create something that will bring in money over time, or you get piggyback income for something you're already doing.

Creative-based income streams work like planting seeds in a garden—you do some work up front and then reap benefits for years to come. This strategy can bring you a steady long-term stream of extra cash from a one-time effort. Examples include:

- Writing and publishing an ebook (Amazon Kindle Direct Publishing, https://kdp.amazon.com, and Outskirts Press, https://outskirtspress.com, are two of the options that make this very easy to do).
- Uploading digital photos to sites like www.istockphoto.com and www.shutterstock.com.
- Creating your own website and packing it with affiliate links (URLs that track back to an advertiser's website, giving you compensation for every reader who clicks through or takes another action on their site) or selling advertising space (this strategy requires a little ongoing work to keep people coming to your website).

Piggyback income streams require less work but also tend to pay less. Examples include things like:

- Selling ads on the side of your car through programs like Carvertise (www.carvertise.com).
- Renting a room in your home through sites like www.airbnb.com.
- Renting your driveway when you're not using it through apps like Pavemint (this works especially well if you live

someplace where it's hard to find parking).

While you probably won't get wildly rich from your passive income streams (though it is possible), they can substantially cushion your monthly cash flow.

START YOUR OWN BUSINESS

Starting a small business (whether you do it full-time or on the side) can be a great way to bring in extra cash while giving you more control over how and when you work, and that's especially true when you launch a home-based business (which keeps overhead costs to the bare minimum). To give your new business its best chance of success, stick with what you know how to do well, and test it out while you still have other steady income.

Beware Cash Drains

Avoid business opportunities that call for large cash investments if you don't have the money saved and earmarked specifically for this endeavor. You don't want your business to bust your budget before you've even had a chance to get started.

Take the time to create a business plan (or at least a miniplan) that defines your business, outlines the products or services you'll provide and their pricing, and estimates revenues (sales) and expenses for the first year or two. To make sure you don't overestimate revenues and underestimate expenses in the beginning, make a worst-case scenario budget based on minimal sales and maximum costs to make sure you can afford to be in business if it doesn't do well right away. Remember to budget for the biggest expense business owners face: taxes. Once you're up and running, you'll find ways to increase sales and maximize profits, adding that reliable extra income into your family budget.

You can get free help starting your company, with everything from creating your business plan to obtaining any necessary licenses or permits. The SBA (US Small Business Administration) offers free seminars, videos, sample business plans and contracts, and low-cost loans to small business owners. You can also tap into decades of experience with SCORE (Service Corps of Retired Executives). This resource offers one-on-one consulting, mentoring services, and expert advice from experienced professionals.

INCREASE CASH WITHOUT WORKING MORE

Money for (Almost) Nothing

Working a second job or taking the time to create passive income streams aren't the only ways to bring in extra cash. There are several ways you can make money with minimal effort after devoting some time to setup (and sometimes not even that). Some of these require you to pony up money to get started, while others require no up-front investment.

You'll see cash coming in pretty quickly from many of these options (such as selling your stuff). Others may take a little time to kick in but then will continue to supply reliable cash over the long haul (such as building up a portfolio of income investments).

SELL YOUR STUFF

There's no limit to the types of items you can sell, as long as they're in good to excellent condition. There are a few different ways you can accomplish this, and most depend on the value of the things you're trying to sell.

Go straight to a specialty dealer for higher-value items such as antiques, jewelry, art, coins, or stamps. You can find them online or by referral from people you know who've sold similar assets. Visit a few reputable dealers who specialize in the specific item, get a firm price from each, and take the best offer.

Auctioning items online is another good choice for selling your things. Use a site like www.ebay.com for less expensive items or www.etsy.com for handmade or vintage items. Check out seller fees, shipping rules, and payment options before listing your items.

For things you want to get rid of quickly, consider listing them in the classified ads on www.craigslist.org. You probably won't get as much money here as you would through an online auction site, but you will get quick cash and you won't have to deal with shipping.

Tax-Free "Income"

Selling your stuff brings in what feels like income, but it's not. Unless you have items (like rare collectibles) that have skyrocketed in value, your stuff will sell for less than you originally paid. That doesn't count as income for tax purposes, so you get to keep every cent your stuff brings in.

If you have a lot of small, low-value household items, go with a yard sale. You'll be able to get rid of a lot of things in a short amount of time and pick up a few hundred dollars in the process. This is the most labor-intensive option, but it works best for items (like single dishes or old Pokémon cards) that someone might want but that aren't really worth shipping.

INCREASE CASH WITH THESE APPS

Apps offer a lot of opportunities to earn rewards—including cash—without expending a lot of effort. In most cases, you're selling marketing information to the app creators and their customers (usually major retailers and marketing firms), a service they're happy to pay you for. Other apps require you to perform services, such as taking surveys or doing simple tasks. Whichever apps you choose to use, you'll have a little extra cash on hand for doing practically nothing. Here's the lowdown on some apps you can cash in on.

Shopping

You can earn money as an undercover shopper with Mobee. This app shows you stores near you that will pay you to shop and comment. You'll be assigned brief shopping missions, answer a quick questionnaire, then earn points that you can trade for gift cards, prizes, or cash.

If you don't want to use credit cards but still want to earn rewards points, use Drop. This app offers points for debit card spending, so you don't have to rack up debt to score points. For every five thousand points you earn, you'll get $5 worth of rewards, reaping benefits from spending within your budget.

Eating

Apps like Fetch Rewards give you cash back on items you buy at the grocery store, and all you have to do is scan your receipt to score gift cards for Sephora, Starbucks, Amazon, and many more retailers. Healthy eaters can get cash-back rewards for buying organic, vegan, non-GMO, and other specialty foods with the BerryCart app.

Wallaby helps responsible credit card users get the most out of their spending. This app tracks all of your credit card rewards programs and lets you know which offers the biggest bonus for any purchase to help you maximize card benefits.

Walking

If you've sworn off shopping, you can earn rewards for walking with Sweatcoin. This app tracks the steps you walk outside (treadmill miles don't count) and turns those steps into "sweatcoins" that you can use to buy things like PayPal gift cards, fitness gear, and even cash.

INVEST IN INCOME STOCKS

Income investing can boost your income with minimal effort on your part. All it takes is a little bit of time and research and some money to invest, and dividends will start pouring in.

What Is a Dividend?

When corporations earn money, they often share those profits with their stockholders (people who own shares of stock in the company) in the form of dividends. Many established corporations regularly pay out cash dividends, making them a reliable form of extra income.

To get started, you'll need to open a regular (as opposed to retirement) investment account. The easiest way to do this is through an online broker (such as E-Trade or Charles Schwab). It takes about fifteen minutes to set up the account and a few days to fund it. While you're waiting for the account funding to come through, do a little research to choose your dividend stocks. Remember to take your overall financial plans and existing portfolio into account as you begin choosing investments.

Look for solid, mature companies with a long history of paying dividends and increasing them regularly (that's called dividend growth). You can find a ton of information online to help you choose the companies you want to invest in. Some of the best free resources to research dividend growth stocks include:

- Kiplinger.com
- Morningstar.com
- SeekingAlpha.com
- Dividend.com
- DividendDetective.com

Creating a collection of solid dividend stocks as part of your overall financial plan can add easy income—and a little more breathing room—to your budget. Make sure to budget a little extra for taxes because dividends count as taxable income.

ALTERNATIVE INCOME INVESTMENTS

You can tap into other types of investments to round out your passive income portfolio. Like stocks, all of these investments have an element of risk, meaning you could lose your money. By including different kinds of investments (a strategy known as asset allocation), you minimize the risk that you'll lose all of your money because, chances are, they won't all tank at the same time. Do your homework, make informed choices, and don't put too much of your money into any single investment vehicle. Follow these basic guidelines, and you'll be able to build reliable passive income streams.

REITs

REITs (real estate investment trusts) work sort of like real estate mutual funds and allow you to invest a little money in a large portfolio of income-producing real estate, mainly residential and commercial rental properties. While many REITs have high initial investment hurdles, Fundrise (www.fundrise.com) lets you invest in a starter portfolio for just $500 and minimal annual fees. You can take your earnings as cash payments every quarter or reinvest to grow your holdings.

Peer-to-Peer Lending

Peer-to-peer lending is a relatively new way to connect borrowers and lenders outside traditional banks. Lenders and investors make money when borrowers pay back their loans with interest, a lot more interest (in the neighborhood of 7 percent to 10 percent) than you'd get if you stashed your cash in a savings account instead. That higher rate also comes with higher risk because some borrowers will default on their loans. You can mitigate that risk somewhat by making several small loans instead of one big loan (for example, four $2,000 loans instead of one $8,000 loan). If you have a high risk tolerance (and you can afford to lose some money) and relish the potential high returns, look into LendingClub (www.lendingclub.com) and Prosper (www.prosper.com).

KNOW YOUR SPENDING TRIGGERS

What Really Sets Me Off

If you often spend more money than you intend to or buy a lot of things you wish you hadn't, it's time to get to the bottom of those spending behaviors. Overspending tends to be tied to emotions, social situations, and chasing a "shopper's high." And while the instant gratification of new purchases feels good, it takes a serious toll on your financial future.

Figuring out what triggers you to overspend can help you take back control and kick this bad financial habit. You'll feel relief when your credit card bills don't send you into a panic, and you won't regret having a closet (or cabinet, or basement) full of things that you don't really want.

SORT OUT EMOTIONAL OVERSPENDING

Emotional overspending tends to fall into one of three categories: guilt, emptiness, or frustration. No matter which emotion drives you, that overspending puts your budget in jeopardy. Looking at the feelings that cause you to spend can help you figure out ways to pause your spending urge and make a conscious financial choice.

Guilt spending is common among parents who feel as if they don't spend enough time with their children, spouses who do a lot of business travel and leave their partners behind to manage everything at home, and grown children who rarely call or visit their aging parents. These situations often lead to guilt spending, where you buy frequent or expensive gifts for the person you feel you've let down.

Emptiness spending kicks in when people feel like something is missing from their lives, and they turn to shopping to fill that hole. Retail therapy offers a temporary sense of happiness and control, and when that fades, the emptiness feels sharper than before.

Frustration spending is often born out of anger and boredom. People get bored and annoyed sitting in waiting rooms or waiting in lines and end up shopping on their phones just to pass the time. Spending can bring a feeling of control to a situation that you don't have any control over.

If you can trace overspending back to any of these emotional triggers, your awareness is the first step toward breaking the negative habits. Look for other ways to deal with your emotions, like finding someone (a friend, a therapist) to talk with or replacing the spending habit with something more productive.

GET A HANDLE ON SITUATIONAL SPENDING

Sometimes you'll find yourself in situations where it feels natural to spend money even if that spending puts you way over budget. This often involves being around other people who are spending money and expect you to do the same.

Common high-spending circumstances include things like:

- Socializing at bars, restaurants, festivals, and other spending black holes
- Going shopping with friends
- Attending weddings, baby showers, and other parties where gifts are expected
- Hanging out with people who frequently borrow money

If you can't or don't want to avoid these situations, be conscious of what you're spending (or lending) and how it will affect your budget, and take proactive steps to make sure you don't overspend. For example, when you know you'll be facing social pressure to spend, leave your credit and debit cards at home and stick with cash, or use tab-sharing apps like Venmo to help make sure you don't get stuck picking up the tab for everyone on margarita night.

Don't Shop Drunk or Hungry

Studies show that shopping when you're drunk or hungry leads to a lot more spending. A 2018 survey (by Finder.com) found that people spent an average of $447.57 extra after drinking. Another study showed that people who shopped hungry spent almost 60 percent more, and not just on groceries (according to a 2015 study published in the Proceedings of the National Academy of Sciences).

DROP A SHOPPING ADDICTION COLD TURKEY

A lot of people get an instant buzz when they spend money. Their purchases just "feel right" in the moment, but they lose their luster as soon as the high starts to fade. Several studies show that shopping can set off a dopamine surge (dopamine is a happiness hormone); we're biologically primed to feel good about acquiring things, which can make it really hard to break this cycle unless you go cold turkey. What's more, a 2015 study by neuroscientist Robert Sapolsky found that online shopping triggers an even bigger dopamine release than in-store buying does.

To bust out of that addictive loop, stop shopping unless you plan to buy something specific that fits into your budget. Avoid stores—even grocery stores—and online retailers when you're alone. Create strict lists before any shopping ventures and stick to them. If it's too hard to control those spending urges even with a buddy present, have someone else do your necessary shopping for you (even online shopping) until you have a better handle on those retail cravings.

WATCH OUT FOR BUDGET BUSTERS

Plugging Up the Leaks

Budget busters typically involve money you spend without realizing it, like autopilot expenses or hidden fees. These costs sneak up on you, draining your checking account and stealing budget space from your goals. They're often small enough that you don't really notice them or consider them when you're looking to make cuts—but these budget busters should be the first expenses you ditch.

Put on your detective hat and find those leaks so you can eliminate them from your budget. You'll find them all over the place, from maintenance fees on your checking account to late fees for overdue library books. With a little bit of effort, you can get rid of these tiny leaks that pad your expenses and open up some room in your budget.

CHECK ON YOUR CHECKING ACCOUNT

Bank fees can eat away at your money, especially when you don't pay attention to them. Most banks charge a long menu of fees for consumer checking accounts, and those fees can add up very quickly. What's worse, when you aren't expecting them, bank fees can even end up triggering more bank fees. You can eliminate a lot of these budget-busting fees by taking simple actions.

- Monthly maintenance fees. Many banks charge maintenance fees of $10 to $12 per month if your balance dips below a preset minimum. You can avoid those fees by making sure you keep that minimum cushion in your account at all times, having the bank waive the fee by setting up direct deposits for your paychecks, or switching to a no-monthly-fee checking account.

- Overdraft fees. When your checking account goes into a negative balance, you'll be charged overdraft fees, and these can run more than $30 each. Make sure you account for everything that drains your account, including automatic payments, checks you've written, ATM withdrawals, debit card transactions, and bank fees.

- ATM fees. Find out if your bank charges for "foreign" ATM transactions (meaning you used a different institution's ATM, like at another bank or a convenience store). Those fees range from $2 to $10 every time you use that foreign ATM. If your bank charges for this, make it a point to only use your bank's ATM, and take out enough cash to last until the next time you swing by.

- Returned-item fees. If you deposit a check that bounces (meaning the person who paid you didn't have enough money in his or her account to cover the payment), your bank will probably charge you a fee, sometimes as much as $15. Not only will that deposit not be in your account, you'll also be out the amount of the fee.

- Paper statement fees. Some banks now charge fees—up to $2 a month!—for mailing out paper statements. Switching to online statements will kill that fee and save some trees.

Bottom line: banks charge fees for pretty much everything. Go to your bank's website and take a look at the schedule of fees (these are sometimes hard to find) so you know exactly what the institution is charging you for.

Check Out the Credit Union

Unlike banks (which answer to stockholders), credit unions answer to their owners—the people who deposit money there. Because of that, they almost always pay higher interest on savings and lower (or no) fees on checking. They also offer their members better loan terms and other benefits.

EXTRA AVOIDABLE COSTS ADD UP

Some costs don't really register; you just pay them and keep going. Sometimes these are expenses that have been on autopilot; others are small fees that crop up now and then. But even small extra costs can end up making a medium-sized dent in your budget when you incur them regularly, so it pays to take steps to avoid them—and that goes double for bigger overlooked expenses.

Examples of extra avoidable costs include:

- Library fines
- "Free trial" subscriptions you forget to cancel
- Memberships you don't use (like the gym)

The worst avoidable cost: late payment fees. Paying these fees is like throwing your money in the trash. If you find yourself consistently missing due dates, make a point of paying bills as soon as they come in or automating payment for bills that are the same every month. You can also set up multiple reminders to help you meet payment deadlines, at least until you're in the habit of making on-time payments all the time.

SET UP SPENDING BARRIERS

Apps and websites make it supereasy to spend money without it even registering. Paying with your phone doesn't really feel like spending money, and neither does one-click online ordering. These "conveniences" rank among the biggest budget busters, and disarming them by setting up spending barriers can make it much easier for you to keep impulse spending in check.

Examples of spending barriers include:

- Deleting stored credit card information on websites
- Removing easy-pay apps from your phone
- Making it physically difficult to pull out your credit card
- Ditching your e-tail memberships (such as Amazon Prime)
- Turning off one-click checkout
- Disabling in-app purchases

Putting up any or all of these barriers will make it harder to mindlessly spend money. When you have to think—even for a few seconds—about what you're buying, you're more likely to nix the purchase and save your money for something you're working toward.

THE PRICE OF PETS

Most people vastly underestimate the cost of having a pet, and that can lead to budget headaches. If this is your first pet (or your first pet of this species), you'll have a lot of basics to buy. On top of those one-time pet setup expenses, you'll have ongoing costs for the life of your pet.

Because they're by far the most common, we'll stick with dogs and cats here. According to the ASPCA (American Society for the Prevention of Cruelty to Animals), these are the average first-year costs:

- Small dog: $1,471
- Medium dog: $1,779
- Large dog: $2,008
- Cat: $1,174

Those first-year costs include things like food bowls, crates and carriers, beds, and adoption fees. Routine ongoing costs include food, vaccines, flea and tick control, and toys. Those ongoing costs—for a healthy pet—can run more than $1,500 a year for a big dog for just the basics. If you need to add in pet sitting or boarding, you'll need to budget even more. And if your pet has a health emergency, expenses can top $2,500 in a single weekend.

If you have pets or are thinking about getting a pet, make sure to work regular and potential emergency costs into your budget. You might even want to set up a separate emergency fund so you never have to think twice about taking your pet to the hospital.

HOLIDAYS TRIGGER OVERSPENDING

Millions of people overspend by hundreds of dollars on holidays, even if they have a special holiday budget in place. The main reasons for this are spending more than expected on gifts, buying extra gifts, and buying snacks while shopping.

To make sure the next holiday doesn't bust your budget, try some of these strategies:

- **Create a holiday budget.** Yes, many people with holiday budgets still end up overspending, but there's a better chance that you won't if you plan your purchases in advance.

- **Use cash.** You can't overspend if you're shopping with cash instead of debit or credit cards.

- **Make gifts.** Handmade presents can be more meaningful to the people you care about (and easier on your budget); you can find dozens of easy-to-make gifts, even if you're not very crafty, at The Spruce Crafts website (www.thesprucecrafts.com) or The 36th Avenue (www.the36thavenue.com).

- **Don't buy cards.** Greeting cards are shockingly expensive, $5 each on average; go with inexpensive blank cards and pen a more personal message.
- **Don't shop hungry.** You should never shop hungry, but it's even more expensive when you're holiday shopping, so fill up before you set foot in the mall.

Taking these steps can help keep your holiday shopping in check so you don't end up blowing your budget and adding to your credit card debt.

DOWNSIZE YOUR BIGGEST EXPENSES

The Machete Method of Cost-Cutting

A lot of budgeting advice focuses on trimming dozens of small expenses, which can be time-consuming and frustrating. Instead, it's often easier to make bigger cuts to a few large expenses than tiny cuts to dozens. In many people's budgets, the three biggest money hogs are housing, transportation, and insurance.

The Biggest Expense Will Surprise You

Your single biggest expense will probably come as a surprise to you: taxes. Taxes eat up more of your income than anything else, and there are so many of them built in to our everyday lives: income tax, payroll taxes, sales tax, gas tax, utilities taxes, and tolls. Together, they can consume 40 percent to 50 percent of your income!

Downsizing is one way—but not the only way—to reduce your housing and transportation costs. Since that can come with other complications (especially when it comes to housing), it may not be the best way to free up money quickly. There are other strategies you can try to reduce these big-ticket expenses and add some room to a tight budget.

TRIM YOUR HOUSING COSTS

Housing costs usually eat up the lion's share of the budget, so making cuts here can go a long way toward freeing up precious cash. If your housing costs take up more than 50 percent of your income, consider finding a more affordable place to live or finding permanent ways to slash the cost, such as refinancing your mortgage or renegotiating your lease.

Home maintenance can also guzzle up a lot of money. Learning how to do some basic home repairs (like patching holes, unclogging drains, and replacing toilet levers) can save you a good deal of money. Taking care of simple repairs yourself lets you avoid expensive professionals who can really drain your emergency fund.

You can also slash your gas and electric bill by using a programmable thermostat. And, according to Energy Saver (www.energy.gov/energysaver/energysaver), you can also trim your utility bills by turning the thermostat up in the summer and down in the winter; you can save as much as 1 percent off your bill for every degree (as long as the change lasts at least eight hours). That website has many more tips for reducing your home energy costs—it's worth a look.

RETHINK TRANSPORTATION

Cars are expensive to own, eating up more of your budget than you realize, especially if you're still dealing with car payments. On top of those payments, you'll also need to cover ongoing expenses. According to AAA, ongoing maintenance and repair costs average $1,186 and gas costs an average of $1,500 per year. Car registration costs, which vary by state, average $145 a year (according to NerdWallet). Plus, car insurance can run anywhere from $1,000 to $2,500 per year depending on where you live, according to ValuePenguin.

If you live in an area where you can walk or bike to work and other essential places (like the grocery store), or if you have a reliable mass transit system in your area, consider getting rid of your car. Then when you absolutely do need a car, go through a car sharing company like Zipcar (www.zipcar.com) or get a ride through Uber or Lyft.

If you absolutely need to own a car, here are some things you can do to reduce car-related expenses:

- Trade in a high-cost or new car for a more efficient used car
- Revisit your car insurance policy and reduce coverage or increase deductibles
- Stay small (smaller cars cost the least to own and operate)
- Rent your car to other people when you're not using it through services like Turo (www.turo.com)
- Use apps like GasBuddy to find the lowest gas prices in your area

Taking any of these steps can save you thousands of dollars every year, opening up a lot of room in your budget to help you meet your goals faster.

SAVE ON INSURANCE

Insurance can take up a big chunk of your annual budget, and it's often an expense that people cut when they're trying to save—but that's a big mistake. A better option is to reduce your insurance costs wherever you can.

The first thing to do is shop around. Insurance companies don't offer loyalty discounts (charging you less because you've been with them a long time), so be open to changing providers to get better pricing.

One quick way to lower your insurance bill: bundle up. Many insurance companies offer hefty discounts for people who bundle services, like getting your homeowners policy and car insurance from the same company. You can also save on monthly premiums for health, homeowners, or car insurance by increasing your deductibles.

When it comes to health insurance, find a policy that covers what you need. You won't end up saving money if your policy doesn't match the way you use medical care. For example, healthy people with no children do fine with low-cost, high-deductible policies, but families with young children may fare better with a higher-cost policy that will save them money on co-pays and wellness visits. You can find health insurance in a few different ways:

- Through the Affordable Care Act (ACA) exchanges at www.healthcare.gov during Open Enrollment periods or when you've experienced certain life events (such as getting married, having a baby, or losing health coverage)
- By contacting any insurance company (such as Cigna or Blue Cross) directly to learn about available plans in your state
- Through a trained, licensed insurance professional who can help you find the best policy (you can find qualified professionals near you at www.healthcare.gov)

REDUCE EVERYDAY SPENDING WITHOUT FEELING DEPRIVED

A Little More Off the Top

Severe spending cuts will undermine your budget, making it impossible to stick with. No one wants to think constantly about where they have to cut back, so look for cuts you won't notice, or at least won't constantly think about.

The fastest way to slash everyday spending is to stop shopping for anything that's not a necessity. If you can't avoid shopping altogether, work on making more mindful purchases. When you take the time to think about what you're buying and what it will really cost you (in terms of your budget), you'll see that you don't want to buy as much as you did before. Until you get there, the strategies mentioned in this section can help you avoid spending money you don't really want to spend.

Don't Fall for Retailer Tricks

Retailers know exactly how to lure you in and encourage you to spend more than you intended or buy things you don't really need. Some of the most common sales traps include:

- BOGO (buy one, get one free) deals
- Percent or dollars-off discount deals
- Free shipping with minimum purchase

When you know which of these or other traps trigger you to spend more, you'll be better able to ignore them.

TRY A CASH CHALLENGE

For one month, use only cash for your day-to-day spending. You'll still pay your regular bills (mortgage or rent, utilities, and debt payments, for example) through your checking account. But for everything else—from groceries to lattes to new shoes—use only cash.

You'll notice that it feels very different to hand over money than it does to swipe a card; it feels like you're spending money. That feeling may make you think twice about some purchases. You'll also know clearly when you're running out of money, and when that cash is gone, your spending for the month has to stop. This forces you to prioritize your spending, and you may be surprised by which regular purchases don't seem important anymore. It also serves as a quick budget reset by highlighting items you can skip without feeling deprived.

UNCOVER HIDDEN COSTS

Hidden costs can bust your budget with stealth expenses you may not realize you're paying. You can uncover these sneaky costs if you know where to look. Then take steps to avoid them going forward, adding more money back into your budget.

Some of the biggest hidden costs culprits include:

- Your cell phone bill, which may be charging for more features, services, and data than you're actually using
- Your checking account, which may be charging you more in fees than you realize, from monthly maintenance charges to "foreign" ATM fees
- Your cable bill, which tacks on fees for equipment, channels you never watch, taxes and surcharges, and "longtime customer" fees (charging you more than new customers for the same service)

If any of your accounts are bloated with these hidden fees, contact the provider to have those charges removed—or consider changing providers (for example, moving your checking account to a different bank) or finding an alternative service (switching to Hulu or Netflix instead of cable, for example).

NEVER SHOP WITHOUT A LIST

Any time you are going to buy anything, whether you're going into a store, hitting up a yard sale, or shopping online, make a list ahead of time. Without a strict list, you may get sucked in by sale prices or discount goods, and you're likely to end up buying something that you don't need. Even the biggest discount isn't a bargain if you buy something you don't need. So before you start shopping, figure out what you need and put it on your list. Then, no matter how great a deal it is, don't buy anything that's not on your list.

SHOP AROUND BEFORE YOU SPEND

When you decide to spend money, especially on a high-ticket item or service, it pays to shop around to find the best deal. Before you walk into a store, go online to find out the price range of whatever it is you want to buy. Check out price comparison sites like www.pricegrabber.com and www.bizrate.com for insights on where you'll be able to find the item at the lowest possible cost.

You might also want to visit Consumer Reports (www.consumerreports.org) to research products while comparing prices, especially for major purchases, so you can make sure you aren't trading quality for savings.

If you decide to buy online to score better pricing, remember to factor shipping costs into your total; shipping costs (especially on large items) can tip the scales in favor of store pricing. If your purchase doesn't qualify for free shipping, see if it qualifies for a rebate at www.freeshipping.com. When a major retailer (such as Walmart or Best Buy) has better pricing online, you can avoid shipping costs by ordering at the lower price online but picking up your purchase at the store.

Another way to lock in savings: buy at the right time by following clearance calendars, guides that tell you the best months to buy specific products. Base your decisions on when retailers offer their biggest discounts. For example, you can find the best prices on refrigerators in May and the best deals on exercise equipment in January. Though the calendars may vary slightly by source, you can find solid information on websites like www.consumerreports.org and www.lifehacker.com.

Other things you can do to spend less on purchases include:

- Price matching (where the store you're shopping in matches the lowest price you can find from a competitor, including websites such as Amazon).
- Rent instead of buy items you'll use only once (like a bridesmaid's dress) or occasionally (like skis).
- Scout the Internet for coupons at sites like www.coupons.com and www.retailmenot.com.
- Use Ibotta (www.ibotta.com) to get cash back on everything from groceries to movie tickets to laptops you buy at participating stores.
- Use apps like LivingSocial, Dosh, and ShopSavvy to find deals on the spot.

All of these will help you reduce spending without sacrificing the things you want. The trick is to only buy what you had planned to buy ahead of time, even if you see a killer deal on something else.

Chapter 6

Take Charge of Your Debt

You are in debt. It's a fact that sometimes feels like a judgment. Being in debt often comes with feelings of guilt, shame, and resentment, and those can keep you from moving forward more effectively. It's important to understand how and why you accumulated more debt than your budget can handle so that it doesn't happen again.

But it's more important to realize that situation already exists, and what matters more is what you do next. When you have a mountain of debt to deal with, it's easy to get discouraged—especially if you aren't seeing huge dips in your debt balance. Remember: every extra dollar you pay makes a dent and reduces your future interest charges, and even simply not adding to your debt is a victory.

RANK YOUR DEBT

Going from Worse to Bad

The best way to understand and tackle your debt is to rank it. There are two factors at play here: debts that are most important to your life and debts that are most harmful to your net worth. In most cases, the most important debt and the most harmful debt will not be the same, so these two lists usually look very different. Still, categorizing your debts in both these ways offers critical insights into the best ways to manage your overall debt.

Regardless of rank, make at least the minimum payment on every debt every month to avoid going into default. Once those payments are completely covered, you'll be able to hone in on your highest-ranked debts for demolition.

Debt on the Rise

Household debt continues to climb at every age. What might surprise you is just how high it climbs, and who owes the most (according to Time magazine):

AGE RANGE	AVERAGE DEBT
Under 35	$67,400
35–44	$133,100
45–54	$134,600
55–64	$108,300
65–74	$66,000
75 and older	$34,500

RANKING YOUR DEBTS BY IMPORTANCE

If not paying a particular debt would have a dramatic negative impact on your life, that debt ranks as a high priority. For example, not paying your mortgage or home equity loan can result in foreclosure; not making your car payment can lead to your car being repossessed. Since you need a place to live and a vehicle to get you to and from work, these are not the payments to skip.

By this standard, your highest-priority debts would include:
• Rent, mortgage, and home equity loan • Car payment(s)

• Utilities
• Taxes

Mid-priority debts won't alter your everyday life, but the consequences of nonpayment could still lead to big problems. This category includes things like student loans and insurance.

The lowest-priority debts won't impact your life today, but they're still important from a financial health perspective. These types of debts tend to come with higher interest rates because creditors know they land low on the priority ladder. This category includes credit cards, gas credit cards, and outstanding medical or legal bills.

RANKING YOUR DEBTS BY HARM TO NET WORTH

When it comes to debts, the ones that do the most harm to your net worth come with the highest interest rates. These are most often debts that aren't attached to a valuable asset. Instead, they're usually for everyday purchases, consumable items, and services—things that don't add to the asset side of the equation. And because of their heavy interest burden, these debts are much harder to pay down.

When you're working toward paying off your debt, these are the types of debt you want to get rid of first. Rank these debts by the highest interest rate to the lowest, regardless of the amount you owe. Once you've paid them off, the money you'll save on future interest payments will now go toward growing your net worth.

OTHER DEBT-RANKING FACTORS TO CONSIDER

There are a couple of other factors you might want to think about when you're deciding the order for paying down your debt, namely your tax situation and your credit score.

Taxes

Certain types of loans come with built-in tax breaks to help offset the interest costs, mainly mortgages and student loans. Interest on other types of personal debt, such as credit cards and car loans, doesn't come with a tax deduction. For many people, it makes sense to put tax-break debts later on the paydown list so they can continue to take advantage of those deductions and lower their tax bills.

Credit Score

Your credit score is another factor to consider. The order of debt paydown impacts your credit score because it affects your credit mix, one of the five factors that goes into the calculation. Credit mix refers to the different types of credit you use, mainly revolving (like credit card debt) and nonrevolving debt (like mortgage, car, and student loans).

If you pay down nonrevolving debt first, that increases the percentage of revolving debt you're carrying (even though it doesn't increase the amount), which can lower your score. For example, if you had $40,000 of nonrevolving debt and $10,000 of revolving debt, your revolving debt would be 20 percent of your credit mix ($10,000/$50,000). Paying off $10,000 of the nonrevolving debt changes that revolving debt portion to 25 percent ($10,000/$40,000).

Five Factors Go Into Your Credit Score

There are five factors that go into determining your credit score, and they don't all weigh the same. Here's a quick look at those factors and their weight: **1.** Payment history: 35 percent **2.** Total amount you owe: 30 percent **3.** Length of your credit history: 15 percent **4.** How much new credit you have: 10 percent **5.** Your credit mix: 10 percent

Keep in mind that you can use whichever method or combination of methods that works best for your situation and goals. As long as you know the types of debts you have, how they fit into your overall financial picture, and how paying them off will affect your situation, you'll be able to make the best choices for your debt paydown plan.

ELIMINATE TOXIC DEBT AS FAST AS YOU CAN

The Debt-Detox Diet

Super-high interest debt, with rates topping 36 percent (and sometimes more than 100 percent), can sabotage your finances and block you from reaching your financial goals. It's extremely difficult to pay off these loans, even if you make regular on-time monthly payments because those payments go almost entirely toward interest. These debts are considered toxic because they do serious harm to your financial position.

Even though paying off these toxic debts feels next to impossible, it can be done. It will take some extreme budget moves, including deep expense cuts and income boosts, but those temporary pains are worth it. Make getting rid of this damaging debt a priority, and watch your budget and net worth benefit.

THE DANGER OF PAYDAY LOAN CYCLES

When you're in an immediate financial fix, a payday loan can seem like a lifeline, but that financial "rescue" comes at a very steep cost. These loans come with extremely high interest rates —the annual percentage rates (APRs) can come close to 400 percent!—that can pull you into a dangerous cycle of needing to borrow more just to get by.

Here's how it works. In exchange for a postdated personal check or an authorization to directly pull money from your checking account, a payday lender essentially gives you an advance on your next paycheck that has to be paid back right away (usually no longer than two weeks). For this convenience, the lender charges you a fee for every $100 borrowed. The way they word it looks as if you're not paying a crazy amount, just $10 or $15 per $100. But it really takes a much bigger toll on your finances.

If the lender charges you $15 for every $100 you borrow, that seems like a 15 percent interest rate. But because the loan has to be paid back in two weeks, the APR is really 390 percent (15 percent divided by 2 weeks times 52 weeks). In comparison, even the highest-rate credit cards don't have triple-digit APRs—and that's part of what makes payday loans so toxic to your finances.

Since you have to pay the lender back when you get your paycheck, you won't be able to use that paycheck to cover your expenses, which forces you into taking another payday loan (and the lender will be very happy to "help you out"). If you can't pay it back, the lender can get a judgment against you and garnish your wages. Breaking the cycle can be very hard, and the only way to get out is to stop borrowing money this way. You'll need to find other ways to get your hands on cash (see Chapter 5 for ideas), even if it means borrowing from family.

AVOID NO-CREDIT-CHECK PERSONAL LOANS

Like payday loans, easy-access personal loans can seem like the way out of an immediate financial problem (like a stack of medical bills). Rather than fixing your finances, though, these instant loans can destroy them, pulling you deeper into debt and making it harder to get ahead. These personal loans are available all over the Internet, and unscrupulous lenders specifically target people with bad credit who are desperate to find a quick cash infusion.

Like payday loans, no-credit-check loans can come with APRs as high as 400 percent. Unlike payday loans, you can pay these loans back over a long period, but that can be impossibly expensive. For example, if you borrowed $1,500 for two years with a 400 percent APR, your monthly payments would be $501, and you'd pay back a total of $12,024—over $10,000 more than you borrowed.

Not All Personal Loans Are Toxic

There are nontoxic personal loans out there, especially for people with good credit who just need a small loan to bridge a temporary financial gap. Make sure you fully understand all of the loan terms, especially the APR and loan period, before you agree to anything. If you feel confused, pressured, or uncertain, walk away.

If you absolutely need to take out a personal loan, do a lot of research to find a reputable lender. You won't get access to the money instantly, but usually in no longer than one week. Start with your own bank or credit union; your institution may be willing to work with you, even when your credit isn't perfect, if you're a longtime customer. Otherwise, look online for more reasonable loan terms, including interest rates not higher than 36 percent. Check out multiple lenders to find the best deal you can get. You can find information about reliable lenders at websites like www.nerdwallet.com or look into peer-to-peer lending at www.lendingclub.com or www.prosper.com.

KNOW THE RULES OF PENALTY RATES

Credit card penalty interest rates can trash your budget indefinitely, turning already troubling debt toxic. This ultra-high rate, usually 29.99 percent, kicks in as a sort of financial punishment when you're more than sixty days late—meaning you skipped two payments—and it lasts for at least six months.

Technically, credit card companies are supposed to reset your rate to the pre-penalty charge after you make six on-time payments and none of them are returned (for example, your check bounces). But there's a catch: they're only required to lower the rate on the balance from before the penalty kicked in. There's nothing to stop them from using the penalty rate for any transactions that took place after it was imposed—and most credit card companies do just that.

Read the Fine Penalty Print

You can find the exact terms about penalty rates right on your credit card issuer's website. The credit card company has to spell out what the rates are, what can trigger them, and whether you'll pay them indefinitely. The fine print will also spell out if a penalty rate on one card can trigger it on other cards you hold from the same issuer.

That means everything you buy going forward is subject to the penalty interest rate forever. In turn, that prompts higher minimum payments (they have to be enough to at least cover the new interest charges). If you've already been having trouble making payments, this will make it worse. The financial strain on your budget will be increased, maybe permanently, and it will be even harder to get out of debt.

PICK A PAYDOWN PLAN

Dig Your Way Out of Debt

Once you've decided to tackle your debt, you'll need to pick the best paydown plan for you. The best plans have you focus on one debt at a time until all debts are paid off. This system works because it's much easier and less stressful to deal with a single debt than a giant mountain of debt all at once.

The two main choices are the avalanche method and the snowball method, and both will help you reach your goal of being debt-free. From a purely mathematical perspective, the avalanche method saves the most in overall interest costs and usually works a little more quickly. However, more people succeed with the snowball method because it offers quicker payoffs to keep motivation running high.

The method that's best for you is the method you can stick with over time. Either one will get the job done. The important thing is to pick your plan and get started.

Do This with Either Plan

No matter which plan you decide to go with, there are three important things you'll need to do:

1. Make an on-time minimum payment on every debt every month.
2. Pick one debt to focus on (the focus debt) for faster paydown.
3. Put every extra penny you can scrape up toward your focus debt.

Number one on the list is crucial. Making late payments or missing payments will increase your debt, making it harder to pay down. To make sure this doesn't happen, set up automatic minimum payments for all of your debts, including the focus debt.

Be Careful with Your Final Payment

Before you make the last payment on any debt, call your creditor to find out the exact payoff amount. Depending on how often interest accrues, that amount may be different than you're expecting, so you could end up with a lingering interest balance.

AVALANCHE

Under the avalanche method, you'll focus on your most expensive debt first. By tackling the debt with the highest interest rate (no matter how small or large the balance due is), you'll end up saving the most money in interest. That's a bonus for your overall finances: every dollar you save in interest payments is another dollar to put toward your goals.

To use the avalanche method, list your debts in order of their interest rates, from highest to lowest. You can usually find that information right on the monthly statement or on the payment coupon. The debt with the highest interest rate will be your focus debt until it's paid off. Then, you'll move on to the new top-rate debt, working on each until they're all settled.

SNOWBALL

The snowball method can work well for you if you're motivated by quick accomplishments (like checking things off a list). The visible progress helps keep you on track and also helps get you in the paydown habit, which can make it easier to stick with your plan when you get down to the larger debts.

Under the snowball method, you'll list all of your debts in order of size, from smallest to largest. You start by chipping away at your smallest debt (your focus debt) first. When it's paid off, you move on to the new smallest debt and keep going in order until they're all settled.

The real beauty of this strategy is that the monthly payments for your focus debts begin to snowball. As each focus debt gets paid off, the money you were using to pay it goes toward the next debt, making those monthly payments bigger—the snowball effect—so the debt gets paid off faster.

SNOWFLAKE

Snowflakes are completely different than avalanches and snowballs: rather than being part of a steady plan, snowflakes refer to extra or unexpected money that you can use to beef up a payment on your focus debt. Snowflakes include things such as your income tax refund, birthday cash, or a $20 bill you find under the seat in your car.

The trick is to put that found money toward your focus debt right away before it disappears into your regular spending. Even though $20 may not seem like a big deal, it will help knock down your balance and interest charges faster, getting you one step closer to debt-free.

MAKE SURE YOUR EXTRA PAYMENTS GET APPLIED TO PRINCIPAL

When you make an extra payment on a debt, you expect that it will go toward the principal balance, but it doesn't always work that way. Directly decreasing the principal balance is best for you because doing that also reduces the amount used in interest calculations, making it easier to pay down your debt faster. Different banks and creditors handle extra payments differently, so find out how the extra money you're sending in will be applied.

With some debts, the creditor applies any extra payments to interest first, and then anything left over can go toward principal. To work around that, include your extra payment with your regular payment to make sure the additional money goes to principal.

Multiple Loans with One Creditor

When you have several loans with a single servicer, common with student loans, the company may spread your extra payment out over all of them instead of applying it all to your focus loan. If you want your creditor to apply your payments to a specific loan, let them know in writing (there's a good sample letter at www.consumerfinance.gov).

Other creditors automatically use extra payments to reduce principal. Here, it doesn't matter if you add to your regular payment or make multiple payments during the month. Just make sure to indicate what you're doing: write "principal only" on your check, check the "extra principal" box on your payment slip, walk into the bank and tell the teller you're making a principal payment, or select "principal reduction" (it may be worded differently) when making a payment online.

Whenever you make extra payments, make sure that they've been applied correctly. Mistakes happen all the time, and a mistake here could set back your debt payoff.

CONSIDER CREDIT COUNSELING

If you're having trouble dealing with your debt (and millions of people do), working with a credit counselor can be a wise move. Trustworthy credit counselors can help you develop a manageable debt repayment plan and map out ways to help you avoid taking on new debt. Their aim is to empower you and teach you how to handle your debt, and they often offer free classes and workshops to help you improve your money management skills.

They work with you to figure out how much you can afford to pay each month and negotiate with your creditors to accept modified payment terms that you can actually meet. This usually involves lowering your monthly payments by getting the creditor to agree to extend your loan term ($200 a month for five months instead of $500 a month for two months, for example). Credit counselors may also get creditors to stop collection calls, lower interest rates, and waive fees—all things that will help you pay off your debt and lower your stress.

That said, there are a lot of disreputable people in this industry, and they prey on people desperate to get their finances in order. Do your homework, and make sure you're dealing with a reputable company before you agree to anything.

HOW TO FIND A REPUTABLE CREDIT COUNSELOR

Most reputable credit counseling agencies operate as nonprofits. They charge very low or no fees to help you put your financial life back together. The trick is to find a credit counselor who's reputable and very good at his or her job.

The best credit counselors will be certified and accredited with one of the main industry associations. You can find reliable information about specific credit counseling agencies from these sources:

- Financial Counseling Association of America (FCAA): www.fcaa.org
- National Foundation for Credit Counseling (NFCC): www.nfcc.org
- Better Business Bureau: www.bbb.org

- US Department of Justice (offers a list of approved credit counseling agencies): www.justice.gov

Watch Out for These Red Flags

Stay clear of any credit counseling companies that:

• Refuse to send you free information about themselves
• Won't tell you their fees up front
• Promise to improve your credit score
• Guarantee that they can stop any lawsuits

If you see any of these red flags, run away.

Finding a credit counselor you can trust can mean the difference between reaching your financial goals and ending up even worse off than you were before.

SIDESTEP DEBT SETTLEMENT SCHEMES

Unlike credit counselors, debt settlement companies try to get creditors to "settle" your debts for less money. This usually involves a big lump-sum payment to clear the reduced debt amount. Not only is that bad for your credit score, it can make it much harder to borrow money down the line. Plus, you may end up owing taxes on the forgiven portion of your debt.

And that's not where the trouble ends. Debt settlement companies often advise you to stop making payments to your creditors and to cut off all communication with them (no reputable company would ever advise that). They may try to collect an up-front payment from you before they get started (which is illegal).

Bottom line: you're better off sidestepping debt settlement completely and going for credit counseling instead.

BE WARY OF CONSOLIDATION LOANS

Debt consolidation loans—especially the ones touted in ads—can trap you in even bigger debt. These "finance company" loans often come with hidden fees, high interest rates, and confusing security clauses that can put your home, car, or savings at risk. They may require you to buy loan insurance, tacking on even more to your loan payments. On top of that, simply having a consolidation loan on your record can make it harder to get credit in the future.

If you absolutely must get a consolidation loan, go through your bank or credit union. The terms will be better than what you'll get from a finance company, and you have a better chance of negotiating new payment terms if you have trouble paying.

AVOID CREDIT REPAIR SCAMS

Criminals often target people who are struggling with debt by offering credit repair deals that sound too good to be true (because they are). If someone is offering you an easy way to improve your credit score (which makes you eligible for better borrowing terms and lower interest rates), it's a scam.

Steer clear of people who tell you that:

- They can get negative information (including bankruptcies or judgments) off of your credit report. You can have inaccurate data removed (see Chapter 8 to learn how), but anything else is illegal.
- You can start over with a new Social Security number and a clean credit slate. Using any Social Security number other than the one you were issued at birth is illegal.
- They guarantee a specific increase in your credit score. While they can tell you about past clients' success stories, no

one can promise that your score will improve at all, let alone by a guaranteed amount.

• You don't need to read the contract before you sign it. ("It's just the standard legal stuff.") A legit contract will disclose all fees, details of the service you're signing up for, and a statement declaring you have three days to cancel the contract, so look for all of that before you sign anything.

The only way to improve a poor credit score is to build up good credit habits. Legitimate credit counselors will help you do that. Everything else is a scam.

Negative Information Hangs Out for a Long Time

Wondering how long negative information will linger on your credit report? General negative information, like late and missed payments, stays on for seven years. Bankruptcies will remain on your report for up to ten years. Anything criminal—like trying to have accurate negative information removed—stays on forever.

WIPE OUT CREDIT CARD DEBT

Don't Be Forever in Their Debt

Millions of people struggle with unmanageable credit card debt, making it impossible for them to build wealth. Among people who carry a balance, the average amount owed is a budget-crippling $15,983 (according to NerdWallet). And using the average credit card interest rate of 16.83 percent (as of June 2018, according to CreditCards.com), one year's worth of interest would top $2,500. As awful as that sounds, the full picture is even worse: if you paid the full minimum payment (2 percent of the balance) every month on time, it would take more than forty years to pay off your card, and you'd pay more than $35,000 in interest—nearly twice the balance.

That's why it's crucial for both your current budget and your financial future to pay off your credit card debt as soon as possible and avoid building it back up. Without all of that money going to fatten credit card company profits, you can quickly build an emergency fund, live without worrying if you'll be able to pay the bills, and sock away plenty of money to meet all of your financial goals.

The hard truth is that the only way to completely wipe out credit card debt is to stop using your credit cards while you're paying down the outstanding balance. Once your debt is paid off and you've built solid budgeting habits, you can begin to use credit cards to your advantage by racking up rewards points and always paying your monthly balance in full and on time.

KNOW HOW CREDIT CARD INTEREST REALLY WORKS

You have a credit card with an 18 percent APR (annual percentage rate), so you expect that you get charged 18 percent interest every year. That's a logical assumption, but it's wrong.

Credit card companies don't charge you interest annually. Instead, they use that APR to calculate a daily percentage rate (also called the daily periodic rate or the periodic interest rate). You can figure out that rate by dividing the APR on your card by 365. For example, if you have a credit card with a 16.99 percent APR, your daily percentage rate would be 0.04655 percent.

That daily percentage rate gets applied to your average daily balance, another credit card complication. Your average daily balance starts with your balance due from last month, then adds purchases and subtracts payments day by day to come up with each day's balance for every day in your billing period (you can find the billing period on your statement). Next, all of those daily balances get added together, then divided by the number of days in the billing period to get the average daily balance.

They calculate the dollar amount of interest you get charged by multiplying the daily percentage rate by the average daily balance, then multiplying that by the total number of days in the billing period.

Keep in mind that credit card companies charge compound interest on your balance. That means you pay interest on interest that was charged in previous months (and sometimes even on previous days depending on how often the issuer compounds interest, which you can find in your cardholder's agreement). For example, if you had a $1,000 balance plus $15 interest charged, the next time you'd be charged interest on $1,015. Because of this compounding, the interest rate you're actually paying is probably more than the APR. The only way to completely avoid credit card interest is to pay your balance in full every month.

Use the Grace Period

Want to use credit cards without paying any interest? Take advantage of the built-in grace period that most card issuers offer. No matter how much you put on the card, as long as you pay your full balance by the due date, you won't be charged any interest at all. But if you pay even $1 less or one day late, the grace period disappears and interest charges will show up.

AN EASY WAY TO LOWER YOUR AVERAGE DAILY BALANCE

Here's a neat trick to reduce the interest charged on your credit cards: make payments as early and as often as you can to make your average daily balance lower. Instead of making one big payment on the due date, split it up into two or more payments sent earlier in the month.

Let's look at an example. Say your last balance was $2,500 and you plan to pay $500 this month. If your card has a thirty-day billing period, and you make one payment on the twenty-fifth day, your average daily balance would be about $2,416. But if instead you paid $250 on day ten and another $250 on day twenty-five, your average daily balance would drop to $2,292. That simple change can reduce your interest charges every month.

MAKE MORE THAN MINIMUM PAYMENTS ON YOUR CREDIT CARDS

Credit card minimum payments are designed to make it take forever to pay off your balance. The longer it takes you to pay, the more money the credit card companies make. So when you go along with their minimum payment scheme, they get all the benefit and you lose money.

Think about this: if you pay just 2 percent of your balance every month (a standard minimum payment), it will take you years to pay it off—and that's if you don't use the card to buy more stuff. That minimum payment barely covers last month's interest charge! By paying more than the minimum—any amount more—you'll get out of credit card debt faster and save money in interest.

That said, it's crucial that you always make at least the minimum payment on time every month to avoid racking up fees, getting hit with penalty interest rates, and tanking your credit score.

TRY TO GET LOWER RATES ON YOUR CARDS

If you've been regularly making on-time credit card payments for at least a year, call your credit card company and ask to have your rate lowered—there's a good chance the company will, and that means you'll pay down your balance faster and save money in interest. If the answer is no, say that you've been thinking about doing a balance transfer to a lower-rate card. If the company's answer is still no, consider doing just that.

AVOID THESE BALANCE TRANSFER TRAPS

When you have very high-rate credit card debt, it may make good financial sense to do a balance transfer—but only in very specific circumstances. In order to pull this off, you'll need to find a card that charges no transfer fees and 0 percent interest for at least twelve months, and you have to be able to pay the balance in full before that free period is up. If you don't, you may be on the hook for interest at the regular high rate from the time you made the transfer on the full remaining balance.

You can also get into trouble if you start using that balance transfer card for purchases. Any payments you make go toward the new purchases first, meaning the balance you transferred is not getting paid down. That can lead to a lot of interest due when the free transfer period ends.

Using a balance transfer wisely, and avoiding all of the transfer traps, can be a great way to speed up your credit card debt payoff, saving you a ton of money in interest and a lot of financial stress.

SHRINK YOUR STUDENT LOANS

Your Mission: Pay Off Your Tuition

Student loan debt plagues more Americans than ever before, tanking their plans for a stable financial future. The numbers are alarming:

- 70 percent of students graduate with debt
- The average person with student loan debt owes $37,172
- The average monthly student loan payment is $393

Those are some seriously budget-busting numbers!

Getting rid of that debt will open the door to financial freedom and help you meet personal financial goals, like saving for retirement or a down payment on a house. If student loan debt has locked you into living paycheck to paycheck, or gotten in the way of your plans, there are several things you can do to get that beast under control.

AUTOMATE AND SAVE

Many student loan servicers will reduce your interest rate by up to 0.25 percent if you allow them to automatically take your payment out of your bank account every month. This strategy has both benefits and drawbacks, so consider it carefully before you sign up.

On the plus side, you'll never have a late payment, so you'll always dodge late payment fees. The lower interest rate will shave hundreds (maybe even thousands) of dollars off the total amount you'll pay over the life of your loan.

On the negative side, you won't be in control of the payments, so you can't skip one if your bank account is light one month. You'll have to make sure your account always has enough cash to cover the payment, or you'll get hit with fees from both your loan servicer and your bank. It also takes about a month to stop the payments if you change your mind.

LOOK INTO DIFFERENT REPAYMENT PLANS

When you first took out your student loans, you were probably shuffled straight into a ten-year standard repayment plan—most people are. With federal student loans, though, standard is not your only option. There are seven other repayment plans available for most loans, and most of them are geared toward fitting your payments into your budget (instead of desperately trying to budget enough to cover the payments). Here are the basics for the seven plans:

1. **Graduated Repayment Plan:** Your payments start out lower than the standard payment and then increase every two years for up to ten years.
2. **Extended Repayment Plan:** Gives you more time (up to twenty-five years) to pay, which lowers your monthly payments.
3. **Pay As You Earn (PAYE) Plan:** Your payment is calculated every year to equal 10 percent of your discretionary income but never more than it would be under the standard plan.
4. **Revised Pay As You Earn (REPAYE) Plan:** Your payment is calculated every year to equal 10 percent of discretionary income (not limited by the standard plan payment amount).

5. **Income-Based Repayment Plan (IBR):** Your payment is calculated every year to equal 10 percent or 15 percent of discretionary income, depending on when you took out the loan, never to exceed the standard payment.
6. **Income-Contingent Repayment Plan (ICR):** Your payment will equal either 20 percent of discretionary income or what a fixed payment would be on a twelve-year loan, whichever is less.
7. **Income Sensitive Repayment Plan:** Your loan term stretches to fifteen years, and your payments increase or decrease every year depending on your annual income.

You can find more details and information about eligibility for these plans at https://studentaid.ed.gov.

What's Discretionary Income?

For federal student loan purposes, discretionary income means the amount your annual income exceeds either 100 percent or 150 percent of the poverty guidelines based on the state you live in and your family size.

A word of caution: by using any of these repayment plans, you'll end up paying more interest over the life of your loan than you would under the standard plan. However, if you're having trouble keeping up with student loan payments, these plans can help you stay on top of them and make monthly payments without busting your budget.

SHOULD YOU CONSOLIDATE YOUR LOANS?

Transforming your multiple federal student loans into a Direct Consolidation Loan may make it simpler to pay down your student loan debt without giving up any of the benefits that come with federal loans (like access to income-based repayment plans). Basically, this process combines all (or some) of your federal student loans into one big loan with one monthly payment to make. Your new interest rate will be a rounded-up weighted average of the rates on your underlying loans. Your loan term will normally be extended, giving you more time to pay, which also makes your monthly payments lower. If you're already in default, consolidating your loans can move you out of that status.

You can do this yourself on the Federal Student Aid website (https://studentloans.gov). The process takes about thirty minutes and is free. Be wary of companies offering to simplify the process for you—those are scams looking to charge you fees for something you could easily do on your own.

For many people struggling to make student loan payments, consolidating their debt makes sense, but there are some drawbacks to this strategy:

- You'll pay more interest, possibly thousands of dollars more, over time because of the longer term and higher overall interest rate.
- Private loans can't be part of a federal consolidation loan, and private consolidation loans almost always have higher interest rates.
- You have to start making payments within two months of consolidating.
- It restarts the payment clock on PSLF (Public Service Loan Forgiveness), which calls for 120 qualifying loan payments.
- Perkins Loans will no longer be eligible for loan cancellation.

Despite the potential drawbacks, consolidating may be right for you if you like to keep things simple. With this plan, you'll have only one loan to track and pay and only one due date to remember. That, in turn, will simplify your budget and help you avoid budget-busting late fees.

Calculating the Consolidated Loan Rate

Here's how to figure out what your new interest rate would be with a federal loan consolidation. Take the balance of each loan and multiply it by its interest rate. Add up those results. Then divide that sum by your total loan balance to get the weighted average rate.

OR SHOULD YOU REFINANCEYOUR LOANS?

Consolidation and refinancing are not the same. Federal loan consolidation basically mushes up your existing loans into a single, stretched-out new loan that still qualifies for special federal loan benefits. Private refinancing trades your existing loans for one new loan with completely new terms, which could include a lower interest rate and shorter time frame, but it loses the benefits attached to any former federal loans.

Depending on your situation, refinancing could make more financial sense than consolidating. If you have a very good credit score, you'll probably be able to lower your interest rate (possibly substantially), which will save you a lot of money over time. You can pick your new loan term, making it either longer (which will lower monthly payments) or shorter (which will increase them), depending on the amount of wiggle room in your budget.

If you're not sure whether refinancing or consolidation would work better for your finances, you can see and compare their effects on the Student Loan Hero website (www.studentloanhero.com) or at NerdWallet (www.nerdwallet.com).

REFINANCE YOUR MORTGAGE

Cut Your Housing Costs

Your mortgage payment is probably your biggest monthly expense (other than taxes, that is). Shrinking this bill will do more to add breathing room to your budget than pinching pennies in other categories. Plus, when you refinance the right way, you will save tens of thousands of dollars over the life of your loan—a real boost to your nest egg.

Before you get started down this road, make sure it makes good financial sense to refinance your mortgage at the current interest rates. You want to make sure your interest rate will be lowered by enough to save you money after you factor in the closing costs. Your best bet is to run the numbers on a couple of online mortgage refinance calculators online. Both NerdWallet (www.nerdwallet.com) and Zillow (www.zillow.com) have easy-to-use tools to give you an instant read on whether the new loan will actually lower your payments and save you money.

Ask Your Lender

You may be able to get your current lender to lower your interest rate, eliminating the need to go through the whole refinancing process. This works best if you have a perfect payment history with the lender and have an excellent credit score. It can't hurt to call and ask; they'll often say yes to keep you from moving to another lender.

Once you've decided that refinancing makes sense for your budget and your financial future, shop around for the best loan terms and lowest closing costs.

REFINANCE THE RIGHT WAY

Refinancing your mortgage can decrease both your interest rate and your monthly mortgage payment, opening up some room in your budget and saving you a lot of money over the life of your loan.

It's also important to avoid potential pitfalls in this process to make sure your budget and your net worth will really benefit from the refinance.

Pitfall #1: Adding time. If you have fifteen years left on your current mortgage, refinance for fifteen years rather than starting over again with a thirty-year loan. Yes, your payments will be higher than if you stretch out the time, but adding time will cost you thousands more in interest payments over the life of the loan, at the expense of your net worth.

Pitfall #2: Getting cash out. Lenders who offer cash-out refinancing frame it as a bonus for you, as extra money you can use to pay down other bills, cover your closing costs, or take a vacation. But all it really does is put you deeper in debt with your house on the line.

Pitfall #3: Underestimating closing costs. Make sure you get a written estimate of closing costs from your lender instead of trying to guesstimate them on your own. This lets you budget for those costs, which usually run thousands of dollars (the average for 2018 was about $7,200 according to ValuePenguin, but varies based on the loan amount and interest rate). Coming up short at closing can kill your refinance deal or force you to put that balance on a credit card.

WHEN NOT TO REFINANCE

In some cases, refinancing doesn't make sense and could, in fact, hurt both your budget and your credit. Make sure you know all the details of your current mortgage, your credit score, and the market value of your home before you apply for a new loan.

If your current mortgage comes with a prepayment penalty (which is unusual but does happen), refinancing can cost a good deal more than you were expecting. These penalties kick in if you pay off your mortgage early and can cost up to 4 percent of your loan balance, erasing the benefits of the refinance.

Another reason to hold off on refinancing: a low credit score. If your credit score isn't excellent, you won't qualify for the lowest possible interest rates. In this case, work on improving your credit score before you apply for a new loan.

Closely connected to this is your DTI, or debt-to-income ratio, which measures the percentage of your income that's eaten up by debt. The maximum DTI to get a qualified mortgage is 43 percent, which means that 43 percent of your gross pay goes toward debt payments. (In some cases, lenders will work with you even if your DTI is 50 percent.) Higher DTIs usually mean higher interest rates, so hold off on refinancing until you can get your ratio down under 36 percent.

Another factor to consider: equity. If you have less than 20 percent equity in your home, wait to refinance. Not only will you get a better interest rate when you have at least 20 percent equity, you also won't have to pay for mortgage insurance.

Chapter 7
Budget Rebuilding Events

Your life circumstances will change, and your budget will need to evolve and adapt when they do to mesh with your new financial reality. With dramatic differences coming in either income or expenses (or both), you'll be better able to face them with a money plan already in place. Some of these changes will be anticipated (like having a child or moving to a new city); others will jolt your finances suddenly (like being fired from your job or getting an inheritance). In any case, when your finances are about to undergo a seismic shift, it's time to recreate your budget.

As part of this budget reboot, you'll retool some of your SMART goals and make room for new ones. You'll take fresh looks at income, expenses, and priorities. And since you're heading into uncharted financial territory, try to prepare for the unexpected costs and cash drains that can accompany your new situation.

YOUR FIRST JOB

Welcome to the Work World

When you first start earning a paycheck, it's really tempting to spend it on all the things you've been wanting—and that's where a lot of people get into trouble. You're expected to know how to manage your money correctly even if no one has ever specifically taught you how to do that. Suddenly, you're responsible for your own bills, and they don't show up until after you've already blown your first paycheck, so you're falling behind right from the outset.

To make sure you don't end up playing financial catch-up and falling ever further behind, you need to create a plan for your money. That starts with knowing exactly how much you'll need to spend on things like rent, commuting, appropriate work clothes, and food along with how much money you'll be bringing in.

BE READY FOR TAKE-HOME SHOCK

That first paycheck may shock you. Between both federal and state income taxes and FICA (a combination of deductions for Social Security and Medicare), your take-home pay will be much smaller—about 25 percent to 30 percent less—than your salary.

If your employer is taking out money for other things, such as 401(k) contributions or health insurance, for example, your take-home pay will drop down even further. Until you know what your paycheck will really look like, you can't budget accurately. When you do, make sure that you base your budget on the actual amount of your check rather than your gross pay.

Figure Out Your Take-Home Pay

You can get an idea of what your net pay will be by using an online paycheck calculator. You can find these handy tools at websites like SmartAsset (www.smartasset.com) and Bankrate (www.bankrate.com).

GET A HANDLE ON YOUR EXPENSES

When you don't have much of a financial history, it can be tough to figure out what your total monthly expenses are. Start with your fixed expenses (meaning they're the same every month), which include things like:

- Rent
- Student loan payment
- Car payment
- Car insurance
- Renters insurance
- Cell phone bill
- Internet
- Streaming services

Next, you'll have to estimate your variable expenses (costs that change all the time). To come up with realistic numbers, do a little investigating. Ask your landlord what typical utility bills run. Ask your parents how much to budget for food. Tap into the experience of friends who've been on their own for longer than you to find out what kind of expenses they have. Then put together your best estimate of total monthly expenses. Don't forget to include things such as commuting expenses, laundry costs, and socializing.

If your monthly expenses are bigger than your monthly take-home pay, you'll need to find a way to bring in some extra money or eliminate some costs. Chapter 5 can give you some practical tips on how to do both.

START PAYING STUDENT LOANS RIGHT AWAY

Now that you have a job, it's time to start paying down student loans—and the faster the better. The sooner you tackle that loan balance, the less interest you'll pay, and all the money you save in interest can be used to fund your goals.

If you can't afford your full student loan payment and your other necessary expenses, look into the loan repayment options discussed in Chapter 6. Do not just stop making your loan payments or your debt will spiral out of control. The interest portion of all of those skipped payments will be added on to your loan balance, and a larger loan balance means higher interest charges. In turn, that means a bigger portion of each payment will go toward interest instead of principal, making it even harder to pay off the balance.

CAN'T AFFORD YOUR LIFE? CHANGE IT NOW

It's easy to overestimate how far your new paycheck will go. If your expenses are outpacing your income, now is the time to make substantial changes so you don't end up buried under a mountain of unpaid bills and expensive debt. The biggest over-expenditure most people face is housing. Do whatever you can to squeeze your housing costs into your budget, rather than trying to force your budget to cover housing costs that you can't afford (since that usually involves running up credit card balances). Whether that means moving, adding roommates, or negotiating with your landlord for a rent reduction, the sooner you do it the better it will be for your financial security.

GETTING MARRIED

Budgeting for Two

Money is often the number one stressor on a relationship, many times arising because of different financial styles when it comes to spending and saving. For example, maybe one of you already works with a budget and has a steady savings habit, but the other is much more casual about money ("When I have money, I spend it"). Or maybe one of you has saved up a substantial down payment for a house while the other has amassed a mountain of debt. Or one of you pays cash for a solid used car and keeps it for two hundred thousand miles, but the other leases a new car every two years. These financial style differences can lead to disharmony unless you address them head-on.

Defusing potential financial landmines before you step on them can head off problems and promote financial harmony. The best way to get everything out in the open and get on the same financial page is to sit down together and create a couple's budget.

KNOW YOUR NEW TOTAL INCOME AND EXPENSES

Believe it or not, 40 percent of couples don't know how much each partner earns (according to a survey by Fidelity Investments). Whether you plan to completely combine your finances or to chip in together from separate accounts, you need to know how much income there is to work with in your budget. Without that information, you won't be able to set SMART goals or create a budget that makes sense. Once you know the total income picture, decide whether you want to combine your assets or maintain separate accounts.

When you mix both incomes together in one joint checking account, your budget will reflect combined income, expenses, and saving. Decide who will be responsible for making sure all the bills get paid and monthly savings goals get met. You'll also need to be open with each other about debit card spending and cash withdrawals to make sure the account doesn't get overdrawn or dip below the bank's no-fee minimum balance.

When you maintain separate accounts, you'll also have separate budgets that feed into the family budget. There are four ways to handle common bill paying, and you'll need to decide which works best for your household.

1. You can each put a portion of your income into a joint checking account and use that money to pay common bills.
2. You can each write a check covering your portion of every common bill.
3. You can designate specific bills to each partner, who will be solely responsible for paying those bills.
4. You can use an app like Splitwise to divvy up household bills and settle up with each other.

If your incomes are dissimilar, divide the bills proportionally. For example, if Partner One brings in 70 percent of the total income, Partner One would pay 70 percent of the common bills.

HIT THESE FINANCIAL HOTSPOTS

A lot of couples have trouble talking about finances, especially when one or both have some troubling or embarrassing money issues. Ignoring these financial hotspots can make them much worse down the line, so grab a drink, set up a no-judgment zone, and share all of your money troubles and bad money habits.

The most common financial hotspots include:

- Defaulted student loan debt
- Overwhelming credit card debt
- History of bankruptcy
- Poor credit score
- Little or no savings
- Binge spending
- Frequent overdrafts
- Day trading

If any of these apply to your new situation, it's important to work together and set up a plan to deal with them before they destroy your joint finances. Include these solutions in your budget goals and take charge of your new financial future.

DEAL WITH THE TOTAL DEBT PICTURE

Debt is one of those issues that people don't like to talk about, but when you're about to combine your financial lives, it's one of the most important points to discuss. Even if you decide to keep your finances separate, the total debt you've each accumulated will affect your future as a couple. Not only will it impact your ability to eventually take on joint debt (should you decide to buy a house together, for example), it can undermine current finances (like paying bills) and saving.

Tackling debt together will help you get rid of it faster—even if you aren't treating it like joint debt and don't both put money directly toward it. For example, if one of you has high-rate debt and the other doesn't, prioritizing that expensive debt in the budget makes good financial sense for the family.

SET JOINT FINANCIAL GOALS

No matter how well you and your partner get along, your pre-couple financial goals may not mesh (or even exist). If you're on opposite sides of the financial map, you'll need to work together to find common ground and joint goals. This can be an extra tough task if one partner doesn't see the point to setting financial goals at all.

Keep Some Money Separate

Even if you and your partner combine all of your finances, it's important for each of you to have some money that's just for you. Your partner will have absolutely no vote as to how that money will be spent, and you never have to explain to each other where that money went.

Clear communication is key here, especially if you have competing goals. Work together to figure out your overall timeline for the things you want to do going forward, such as going to grad school, buying a house, or retiring by the time you're fifty.

Once the two of you agree on a set of goals, follow the SMART goal guidelines laid out in Chapter 1, then include line items to help you meet those goals in your family budget.

WORKING THE BUDGET TOGETHER

Once you've created your couple's budget, you have to follow it . . . together. The two easiest ways to do this, especially in the beginning when you're getting used to being accountable to someone else, are to use only cash for purchases and to get a couple's budgeting app such as Honeydue or Honeyfi. These strategies will help you track all of your spending and make sure you don't go over budget accidentally.

Having regular budget meetings will also help the two of you be in better financial sync while you're getting used to this new "we" money. Use this time to review your spending categories to see how much room is left in each and measure progress toward reaching your family goals.

BUYING A HOUSE

Entering the Money Pit

New homeowners—and their bank accounts—are often shocked by the ongoing expenses tied to their houses (they're not called "money pits" for nothing). That's on top of the one-time costs you'll incur to secure a mortgage and close the deal, which will run several thousand dollars. You'll also want to budget for moving expenses, temporary storage costs, pre-move cleaning services, and any necessary furnishings you don't already have (anything from a washer/dryer to a kitchen table).

Once you've settled in, you'll have ongoing maintenance costs, occasional repairs, and new insurance issues, which can send your budget into overload. Retooling the budget to account for the new spending can help make sure that buying a house doesn't leave you living paycheck to paycheck or put you deeper in debt.

AIM FOR A 20 PERCENT DOWN PAYMENT

Having a down payment of at least 20 percent of the home sales price is a shrewd financial move for several reasons—and all of them will benefit your financial picture over the long run.

1. You'll qualify for better loan terms and a lower interest rate, which can save you thousands of dollars over the life of your loan.
2. You won't have to pay private mortgage insurance, or PMI (which protects only the lender if you're unable to make loan payments), which can cost about 1 percent of your

mortgage balance annually, usually added into your monthly mortgage payment.

3. A higher down payment means a lower loan balance, which reduces the portion of every payment that goes toward interest.

4. An equity safety net, which will protect your overall finance fitness if home prices drop dramatically.

You can get a mortgage with a smaller down payment, especially if you have a high credit score and a low debt-to-income (DTI) ratio, but it's in your best financial interest to save up the 20 percent before you go home shopping.

BE PREPARED FOR CLOSING COSTS

The process of buying a home comes with a lot of costs to seal the deal, and they all have to be paid at closing time. These costs typically work out to about 3 percent to 5 percent of the sales price (unless you're paying the realtor fees, and then it can run up to 10 percent). Standard closing costs can vary widely from state to state, and they usually include:

- Legal fees (if you worked with a lawyer)
- Mortgage taxes
- Transfer taxes
- Recording fees (the cost for a county clerk to record your deed transfer)
- Title insurance (which covers the deed for your home)
- Prorated costs for property taxes and homeowners association dues (reimbursing the seller for expenses they prepaid)
- Realtor fees (if they're not being covered by the seller)

Find out what your estimated total closing costs will run and make sure to save up enough cash to bring to the closing table.

BE READY FOR MORTGAGE PAYMENT ADJUSTMENTS

Millions of Americans have adjustable rate mortgages (ARMs, also called variable rate mortgages), a type of loan where the interest rate changes regularly, and usually upward. Lured in by lower initial interest rates and payments, these homeowners are often unprepared when their monthly payments start adjusting, almost always increasing. When they can't meet the full new monthly payment, the shortfall gets tacked back on to the loan—the loan balance increases even though they're making payments (a situation called negative amortization).

Here's how that happens. Payments are steady for the introductory fixed period of the loan (newer loans usually start adjusting after three or five years). Then interest rate adjustments kick in based on a formula spelled out in the mortgage agreement, such as 1 percent plus the prime rate (or another rate, like the rate on Treasury bonds). So, if the prime rate (the rate that banks charge their very best customers—like other banks—for loans) was 4.75 percent, your new interest rate would equal 5.75 percent.

When the interest rate changes, your monthly payment changes as well, almost always increasing. Even though those adjustments are usually capped, meaning the rate or payment can't change by more than a certain amount each time, many homeowners' budgets can't cope with the payment increase.

Even Fixed Rate Mortgage Payments Can Increase

If your property taxes and homeowners insurance are included in your monthly mortgage payment, be prepared to watch that payment go up every year. Property taxes and insurance premiums almost always increase, often causing your escrow account (a sort of mortgage savings account that holds the money for those expenses until they come due) to go negative. That prompts an increase in the mortgage payment, which could easily strain your budget.

To avoid that budget-busting issue, make sure you know exactly when your payments will adjust and what the maximum adjustment could be. Include that maximum in the budget, and you'll be prepared to handle the next increase no matter how much it is.

PLAN ON MAKING A LOT OF REPAIRS

When you rent, your landlord foots the bill for home repairs. When you own your home, all of those expenses land on you, and they almost always cost more than you expected. The first place to look to get a handle on upcoming repairs: your home inspection report, which details the condition of the house and major appliances.

Other things to consider when you're trying to estimate repair costs include:

- How old your house is (increase your repairs estimate for every ten years)
- The climate where you live (extreme weather increases your costs)
- The home's general condition (add more for a fixer-upper)
- The age and condition of the roof

If you're unsure of how much to budget for home repairs, start with this rule of thumb: every year, add 1 percent of the price you paid for your house into your budget to cover repairs.

Leave Room for Upkeep Expenses

Repairs aren't the only expenses you'll be responsible for when you own instead of rent. You'll also have to pay for routine maintenance costs to keep your home safe and in good shape. According to a survey by Bankrate.com, homeowners pay (on average) $2,000 a year on maintenance services. Even if you take on some of the jobs yourself, you'll still need to budget for equipment, tools, and supplies to get those jobs done.

Regular home maintenance costs include:

- Pest control
- Yard maintenance
- Security system

If you're unsure of how much to budget for ongoing maintenance, go with the 1 percent rule. As you experience how much maintaining your house actually costs, adjust that estimate to reflect your real expenses.

HAVING KIDS

Gear Up for the Costly Cute and Cuddly Crowd

Babies bring unlimited joy into your life, along with major changes and a multitude of expenses. Children are, hands down, the biggest budget busters there are. According to the most recent Consumer Expenditure Survey from the United States Department of Labor, it will cost around $285,000 to raise a child from birth through age seventeen (and that doesn't even include college costs!). That's the average for covering the basics (shelter, food, clothing, medical care, and child care). If you want to add in some "extras" (like college savings, birthday parties, smartphones, and sports gear), your costs could be more than doubled.

Kids Getting Paid

The American fourteen-year-old gets an average allowance of $12.26 a week (according to a survey by RoosterMoney). That shakes out to almost $640 a year, and most of it gets paid through apps like RoosterMoney and FamZoo rather than in cash.

No matter how much you spend on your kids, it'll be more than you're spending now, so make sure to prepare—with extra savings and a revised budget—to keep your family on sound financial footing.

MAKE TWO BABY BUDGETS

Almost everyone underestimates how much they'll spend on their baby during the first year alone. The most common guesstimate is about $5,000, but the actual average first-year cost is closer to $21,000.

That's because babies (especially first babies) require a lot of gear and supplies. You'll need to make a lot of one-time purchases as well as dozens of ongoing purchases. The easiest way to budget for all of this is to deal with the items separately: create a stand-alone budget for the single purchases and incorporate the ongoing expenses into your regular monthly budget.

Some things many expectant parents forget to budget for include:

- The drop in income during parental leave
- The cost to create or update a will
- Extra cleaning costs (especially laundry!)
- A pediatric medicine kit
- Getting or increasing life insurance

You can find baby prep lists online that will help make sure you include everything you might need (from breast pumps to safety gates). Check out websites like www.thebump.com and www.babycenter.com to find checklists and calculators that will help you account for all of the costs.

Three Ways to Keep New Baby Costs in Check

Once you've made your baby budget, find those places where you can minimize costs. You can keep costs under control by:
1. Shopping around ahead of time to take advantage of sales and bulk buying for items you're going to use a lot of (like diapers, formula, and onesies).
2. Buying some of your baby gear used instead of new (the baby won't notice!).
3. Hitting up tag sales and resale shops for deep discounts on baby furniture, clothes, and toys.

KNOW YOUR NEW MEDICAL COSTS

Even an uncomplicated textbook pregnancy and delivery costs thousands of dollars. Plus, even the healthiest infants go to a lot of well-baby visits. Make sure your budget includes enough space for these new costs by contacting your service providers well ahead of time.

If you have health insurance, call your provider to find out how much your pregnancy, childbirth classes, delivery, and baby visits are going to cost you in deductibles and co-pays. Then, find out how much your regular premiums will increase because of the extra person who will be covered by your policy. Be aware that most policies give you thirty days from the birth date to add your child to an existing policy, so don't delay; babies get sick a lot, and you don't want to rack up doctor visits without coverage.

If you don't currently have medical insurance, call your OB-GYN, pediatrician, and local hospital to get estimates on how much having a baby and keeping him or her healthy will cost. If you don't have enough cash on hand to cover the labor and delivery costs all at once, find out whether the hospital offers a payment plan that your budget can manage.

CHILD CARE, ACTIVITIES, AND BIG-KID GEAR

Child care is often the largest cost for families with a young child or young children, easily topping $8,000 a year if you use a daycare center full-time, according to Care.com. Luckily, this cost disappears when your child is old enough to attend school (if you go with public school). At the same time, costs for after-school care and activities will start to kick in.

What about Summer?

Don't forget to include costs for things like pool membership, summer camps, educational bridge programs, beach passes, day trips, or extra child care in your budget. Even families with a stay-at-home parent should budget for some summer activities.

If your family budget is already stretched thin, you'll have to make some hard choices about activities, such as limiting each child to a single activity. Consider low-gear activities (like martial arts) over high-gear activities (like lacrosse) to keep from going over budget.

START SAVING FOR COLLEGE

With college costs spiraling out of control and student loan debt crippling graduates' financial futures, getting a head start on college savings can make all the difference for your child. Even community college and state schools can end up costing thousands of dollars—and that's without adding in room and board for students who choose to live on campus. Total college costs include:

- Tuition and fees
- Room and board
- Books
- Transportation
- Laptops (or tablets)

To minimize the need for student loans, start saving for college costs as soon as you have a child. Saving as early as possible lets you take the most advantage of compounding, especially if you use a tax-advantaged account such as a Roth IRA or a state-sponsored 529 college savings plan. Be aware that any money in 529 plan accounts counts when financial aid packages are calculated, while money in Roth IRAs does not.

DON'T STOP SAVING FOR RETIREMENT

A lot of parents (especially single parents) put their retirement savings on hold. They shift all of the money they were contributing to their 401(k) into college savings, which sounds like a good idea but is a huge financial mistake.

Your retirement funds will lose more than just those contributions. They'll lose the momentum of compounding, and you won't be able to recover that lost growth. If you don't have enough money to save fully for both retirement and college, split your contributions, with the much bigger piece going toward retirement. After all, you can borrow money to cover college costs, but you can't borrow money to fund your retirement.

FINALLY DEBT-FREE

Pop the Champagne! (But Don't Run a Tab)

The day you make your last debt payment feels amazing: no more worrying about minimum payments and late fees, no more stressing about how you'll ever get out from under it. But it can also be a dangerous time, budget-wise. The cash that used to go toward debt has to go somewhere else now, and those feelings of freedom can lead to impulsive spending, which can quickly turn into overspending that lands you back in debt.

A better choice: redesign your budget to capture wealth-building goals and to make sure you stay out of debt for good.

STAYING OUT OF DEBT DOESN'T HAVE TO MEAN NEVER USING CREDIT

Everyone tells you how to budget for paying off debt, leaving you on your own once you've done that. Creating a post-debt budget helps make sure you don't ever build up that level of debt again, even if you decide to continue using credit. Now that you fully understand the emotional and financial costs of being in debt, you can make a plan to use credit responsibly, as a financial tool that benefits you rather than the lenders.

Take these steps to make sure using credit doesn't send you back into a stressful debt situation:

- Keep your credit utilization under 15 percent (which means use only 15 percent of your available credit)

- Only use credit for things you can afford to buy right now with cash, and save that cash to pay your credit card bill when it comes
- Know how much you owe all the time (especially important if you're sharing finances with a significant other)
- Keep room in your budget to pay credit card bills in full every month (if you can't, stop using credit cards)
- Avoid falling into spending traps by staying aware of your spending triggers

Good spending and budgeting habits got you out of debt, and now they will help keep you out of debt as long as you keep following them.

STAY ON TOP OF YOUR CREDIT SCORE

Most people are shocked to find that paying off debt makes their credit score lower, at least at first. One reason that can happen is because of the change in your credit mix as you pay off specific debts. Other things that can cause your score to drop include:

- Not using any credit
- Mistakes on your credit report
- Canceling credit cards that you paid off
- Lowering credit card available credit

Those last two have the effect of increasing your credit utilization ratio, a measure based on your total available credit (you can find details on credit utilization in Chapter 8). When you decrease your available credit, this ratio automatically increases, which can ding your credit score.

Even if you don't plan to borrow money again (ever), it's a good idea to maintain a good credit score because it can affect other things like getting a job and buying life insurance. If you do borrow again, having an excellent credit score will make you eligible for the best possible terms. You can maintain a healthy credit score without going into debt by regularly charging a small amount on a credit card, then paying the balance in full every month.

USE YOUR BUDGET TO PRE-FUND YOUR GOALS

The best way to not run up debt is to pay for things with cash—and you can pay for anything with cash if you plan ahead. It's the exact opposite of borrowing money to buy something, with one huge additional benefit: you won't lose any money to interest payments. Another potential benefit is that paying cash can often result in discounts, saving you even more money. By pre-planning your big purchases, you'll eliminate the urge to spend more than you intend. It's very easy to overspend when you're signing a loan agreement or swiping a credit card, but not when you have cash in hand.

Instead of making your next big purchase with credit and then making years of monthly payments, you make the payments to yourself before you buy and then pay cash for your purchase. The setup here is simple:

1. Create a SMART goal for whatever you want to buy that includes a specific dollar amount and a time frame. (I want to buy a used car for $10,000 in two years.)
2. Figure out how much you need to save monthly to meet that goal ($10,000/24 months = $417 per month).
3. Open a dedicated savings account and name it. Studies show that naming an account makes it less likely you'll withdraw money for something else.
4. Set up automatic monthly transfers into the dedicated savings account.

At the end of your preset time frame, you'll have the cash you need to get what you want without taking on any debt. If you have multiple goals that overlap time-wise, set a plan to pre-fund all of them so you don't have to miss out on anything you want.

SWITCH FROM DEBT PAYDOWN TO WEALTH BUILDUP

To supercharge your wealth-building goals, take the money that would have gone toward debt payments and instead put it into saving and investing. You're already used to living without that money in your budget, making it even easier to redirect it into savings and investment accounts.

This is the time to create passive income platforms and build a portfolio of investments that will provide income streams with growth potential (you can find dozens of suggestions in Chapter 5). Not only will this secure your financial independence and security, it will steadily add to your net worth and fund your future.

GETTING DIVORCED

Stability after Separation

During a split from a spouse or significant other, your finances are especially vulnerable, even when you're parting on good terms. Sorting out combined finances can be tricky, both logistically and emotionally. You'll have to make some tough decisions, including things like how you'll split joint assets, where you'll live, and how your children will be supported financially. All of these factors will play a part in creating a breakup budget that will help keep your financial situation in the best possible state.

As soon as you split, you'll figure out a temporary living budget to cover your most immediate and critical expenses. Once the financial dust has settled and you know how things (including retirement accounts, investments, and debt) have been split, it will be time to create SMART goals and a more permanent budget to reflect your new single life.

PLAN FOR LEGAL FEES

The biggest budget buster during a split-up is the legal fees. Even for a simple divorce, the average legal fees run up to $5,000 for each person. A more complicated divorce (with contested finances, custody issues, etc.) can end up costing $20,000 or more (again, for each of you). Nearly all of those costs are paid directly to lawyers. Actual court costs for filing a divorce run only a few hundred dollars in most states.

If your divorce is uncontested and straightforward, consider filing without using lawyers. That doesn't mean you have to go it alone: divorce mediators can help resolve any sticky issues at a fraction of the cost of attorneys.

A messy divorce, on the other hand, usually requires lawyers to sort things out. You can still minimize your legal bills here by doing as much of the legwork on your own as possible. Keep meetings short by coming prepared with copies of any documents they ask for (such as bank statements). Try to stay focused and unemotional when you're with the lawyer to keep the meeting on track.

FOR A STAY-AT-HOME PARENT

Some of the biggest fears in financial separation involve parents who haven't been working outside the home because they've stayed at home to raise children. If this is your situation, creating a budget can help calm those fears. Not knowing how you'll be able to handle the finances in the months and years ahead can be paralyzing; taking charge of every aspect you can is empowering.

Start by making a new pared-down family budget so you'll know approximately how much money you need to get by each month. Be ready to live on substantially less money than you're used to, as now the single family income will have to pay for two households. Then, if possible, sit down with your spouse (and possibly a mediator) to determine what funds will be available to cover your household expenses until you're able to bring in enough income to live on. And start figuring out ways you can earn money from home to minimize the initial changes. Trustworthy websites like www.flexjobs.com specialize in legitimate work-from-home opportunities and offer work for a wide variety of skills and skill levels. You can also find some money-making ideas in Chapter 5.

CHILD SUPPORT FIGURES INTO YOUR BUDGET

When one parent will have primary physical custody of the children—meaning they'll live with that parent for more than 50 percent of the time—the "live out" parent normally pays child support as his or her contribution toward the children's living expenses. If you are the parent who will be paying child support, add it to your budget as a high-priority ongoing expense to make sure that your children won't be deprived of any essentials.

A Word about Alimony

Alimony, or spousal support, is sometimes used where one spouse hasn't worked (usually to care for children) by agreement. Alimony is typically granted only with long-term marriages and for a specific time. If you're ordered to pay alimony, it's a legal obligation like any debt and belongs in your expense budget.

If you are the parent receiving child support, don't rely on it as your main source of income. Remember, just because something is written into your divorce agreement doesn't mean it will actually happen. And even in friendly divorces, circumstances can change: the paying spouse can lose his or her job, become disabled, or die. Accept the support when it comes, but budget as if it won't.

WATCH OUT FOR DEBT TRAPS

The mechanics of splitting joint debt aren't as simple as they appear. Even when you've agreed on who will be responsible for which debts and put that into a written agreement, creditors aren't bound by that. To be clear: if your ex stops making payments and defaults on debts that were taken on while you were together, creditors can hold you responsible for those payments. You can protect yourself against this possibility by adding a "debt cushion" savings account into your budget.

Other things you can do to protect your budget and your credit score include:

- Close all joint accounts, including bank accounts and (especially) credit cards
- Remove your ex as an "authorized user" from any accounts in your name
- Remove your name from joint financial agreements, including leases and utility bills
- Refinance any joint loans (such as a mortgage or car loan) in just one of your names
- Check your credit report for any joint obligations you may have missed, forgotten (like unpaid medical bills), or didn't know about

Make on-time payments every month for the debts you've agreed to take on. This is crucial to building up your new solo credit history.

THE SINGLE-AGAIN BUDGET

Now that you're on your own, your income and expenses are dramatically different than they were as part of a couple. If you weren't in charge of the finances before, taking control can feel unnerving at first. The key is to start with building a basic budget that takes your new cash flow into account.

Add up all of your reliable income sources, which may include child support and alimony if you're already receiving them. List your fixed expenses (like rent and loan payments). For your variable expenses (such as groceries), you'll have to estimate for the first few months, but soon you'll have a spending history to track and look back on so you can better account for those expenses.

Creating this game plan will help you gain financial confidence and set you up to thrive. It will also give you a sense of control over your money at a time other parts of your life may feel unsettled. Once you have a handle on the day-to-day money management, you'll be able to set reasonable SMART goals to move you toward financial freedom.

NEARING AND ENTERING RETIREMENT

Hitting the Home Stretch

Financial priorities change dramatically as retirement grows near. After all, the money you've saved has to be enough to cover your expenses for the rest of your life. Saving as much as possible before retirement takes precedence over spending, with one exception: taking care of debt. These super focused priorities mean retooling your pre-retirement budget.

Once you enter full-blown retirement, you'll tweak your budget again to factor in your new income streams and expenses. Doing this will help make sure you get to do all of the things you've dreamed of doing, will keep you from spending too much money too fast, and will remove the stress of wondering whether you'll be able to make your savings last.

TAKE ADVANTAGE OF CATCH-UP CONTRIBUTIONS TO BOOST SAVINGS

If you're at least fifty years old, you're eligible to make extra tax-advantaged contributions into your retirement accounts every year. By taking advantage of the catch-up contributions, you'll beef up your retirement savings and create more opportunity for earnings growth.

As of 2018, you can add an extra $6,000 to contributions into employer-based plans, such as 401(k) or 403(b) plans. You can contribute an extra $1,000 to IRAs (both traditional and Roth).

And, yes, if you put money into an employer plan and an IRA, you can make catch-up contributions for both.

Along with that savings boost, take a look at any fees that might be eating away at your nest egg, including ones that might be hidden inside your 401(k) plan. For example, 401(k) plan management fees can run as high as 1 percent, which doesn't sound like much, but that's coming out of your savings —and reducing your earnings—every year. Every dollar you're paying in fees costs you even more because that dollar is no longer working for you. Give your retirement accounts a "fee checkup" by using an online fee calculator on sites like www.personalcapital.com or www.blooom.com.

DOWNSIZE DEBT

Credit card, student loan, car, and mortgage payments can cripple your retirement budget. The more you're putting toward debt, the faster you'll run through your nest egg and the less money you'll have to spend on living your life. Before you get there, take giant steps toward paying down debt and avoid taking on more.

More than 60 percent of people over sixty have debt to deal with, and the median amount they owe is about $40,900 according to the National Council on Aging. That's a lot of debt to manage while your income stream is dwindling. To keep debt from damaging your plans, try to pay down as much of your debt as possible, especially the big three: mortgage, student loans, and credit cards.

Housing is normally the biggest expense in retirement, eating up more than 30 percent of the annual budget. Unless you pay off your mortgage, that is. That eliminates one of your biggest expenses, freeing up a lot more cash for other things and greatly reducing the risk that you'll ever lose your house. Plus, in case of a serious financial emergency, you can tap into your home equity.

Student loans can also blow up your retirement budget in more ways than one. In addition to dealing with hefty monthly payments, falling behind on student loans can result in reduced Social Security benefits.

When you're living on fixed income, it can be harder to pay more than the minimum due on credit cards. Because the interest rates on credit cards far outpace average investment returns, that debt sucks up an outsized portion of your nest egg. Pay off as much credit card debt as you can before retiring, and be very careful not to add any more.

BUDGET TO MAKE YOUR SAVINGS LAST

Once you retire, both your income and expenses will look different. On the income side, you'll start receiving Social Security and pulling money out of your retirement accounts. On the expense side, you won't have all the costs associated with working—such as commuting, daily lunches out, or dry-cleaning—but you'll have new expenses tied to whatever you decide to do next.

Compounding Continues

Your money won't stop working for you once you retire. Your retirement accounts are designed to last for twenty years or more, so keep the long-term portion (any money you won't need in the next three to five years) in high-return investments (like stocks) to take advantage of continued compounding and growth.

Your income will come from a combination of Social Security benefits, retirement savings, and any additional income streams that you've set up. Many people also find they miss work, and they look for job opportunities that fit into their new lives and bring in some more cash. Include all of your reliable income in your retirement budget.

Then, turn to your expenses. First, look at the essential expenses that won't be changing: housing (including property taxes, insurance, and utilities), food, transportation, and loan (or other debt) payments. Next, budget for Medicare or other health insurance, expected healthcare costs, and estimated income taxes (it pays to meet with an experienced tax accountant during your first year so the taxes don't catch you off guard). After that, look back at your pre-retirement budget for any other expenses that might carry over, such as gifts and gym or club memberships, and drop any that no longer apply. Finally, include plenty of fun in your budget. Whether you're hoping to travel, explore new hobbies, go to every home team baseball game, or spend more time at the opera, add those costs into your plan.

Once this is all laid out, you'll be able to see clearly whether your new income can support the lifestyle you want. You may need to reallocate some of your money to fund your new life. That might mean downsizing your house to pay for world travel or giving up your gym membership so you can take in more baseball games.

DON'T UNDERESTIMATE HEALTHCARE COSTS

According to the Fidelity Retiree Health Care Cost Estimate, the average healthy couple can expect to spend around $280,000 for medical expenses during retirement—and that doesn't include long-term care. Healthcare is one of the top budget drains for most people, and costs are expected to keep going up.

The most important thing you can do to keep healthcare costs from decimating your budget is to plan for them based on how much medical care you use now. Adjust your current costs for inflation (use 3 percent to 4 percent a year) to get a more accurate picture. Add in expected Medicare premiums, which run at least $1,600 per person per year. Also include extra for surprise costs, like needing a replacement crown. To help you estimate, AARP has an online retirement healthcare cost calculator (www.aarp.org).

One thing you can do to keep healthcare costs from taking over: fully fund a tax-advantaged HSA (health savings account). In order to use an HSA, you have a high-deductible health insurance plan—and it's worth it. The money you put in is either pre-tax (if it's through an employer plan) or tax-deductible, and all the earnings are tax-deferred, similar to a traditional retirement savings account. And as long as you use the money for medical costs (at any age), your withdrawals are 100 percent tax-free. You can even use your HSA money to pay your Medicare premiums.

WHEN TO START SOCIAL SECURITY AND MEDICARE

Social Security and Medicare will play a part in your retirement budget. Both programs come with different rules and deadlines that you need to know ahead of time so you can plan effectively.

You can claim Social Security benefits any time between ages sixty-two and seventy, and your start date will have a big impact on your monthly benefit. If you start before your full retirement age, or FRA (which you can find at www.ssa.gov), your monthly benefits will be reduced. Waiting until your FRA scores the full monthly benefit. But if you wait until age seventy, you'll get even more. In fact, if you start at age seventy rather than at age sixty-two, your monthly benefits will be up to 76 percent bigger—giving your budget a lot more breathing room.

For Medicare, the rule is tighter: you have to sign up when you hit age sixty-five to avoid a late payment penalty that increases your premiums forever. If you're already signed up for Social Security at age sixty-five, you'll be enrolled automatically.

Medicare has four parts:

- Part A covers inpatient hospital and hospice costs
- Part B works like basic medical insurance
- Part C works like premium medical insurance
- Part D covers prescriptions

Of those, only Part A is free; everything else comes with premiums that run more than $130 a month each, per person. When you sign up, you'll be automatically enrolled in Parts A and B. You can decide to opt out of Part B or opt in to Parts C and D based on your medical situation. To sign up for Medicare or to learn more about the programs and premiums, visit www.medicare.gov.

USE SAVVY STRATEGIES TO MINIMIZE TAXES

Taxes suck up a surprising amount of retirement income. As soon as you start pulling from retirement accounts, all of those deferred taxes will kick in. By carefully planning your withdrawals, you can minimize their tax impact and maximize your retirement savings.

- **Step one:** Take your required minimum distributions (RMDs). These are the funds that come from retirement accounts like traditional IRAs and 401(k) plans, where you saved pre-tax money. Once you hit age seventy-and-a-half, you have to take withdrawals—at least the RMD—every year to avoid steep tax penalties. The IRS website (www.irs.gov) has an RMD calculator so you can make sure to not come up short on these distributions.

- **Step two:** Pull money out of your regular taxable investment accounts. You're paying taxes on the earnings here whether or not you withdraw the money, so you might as well use it.
- **Step three:** Take money out of your tax-free accounts, such as Roth IRAs. These withdrawals won't have any impact on your tax bill.
- **Step four:** Pull any additional funds you need out of your traditional retirement accounts. You'll pay taxes on these withdrawals too.

Steps three and four can be reversed, depending on your specific tax situation. If you're paying minimal income taxes, it may pay to take money out of tax-deferred accounts before tax-free accounts to grow those future tax-free earnings.

Chapter 8

Don't Let Emergencies Derail Your Plans

If you're experiencing a severe financial setback, you're not alone and your finances will recover. No matter what caused the disaster—a market crash, medical bills, job loss—there are specific steps you can take to restore your financial security and begin moving toward prosperity. The most important step is the first one: accept your situation (without judgment) for what it is. Looking backward, assigning blame, and beating yourself up won't change anything. Moving forward will.

Now you're ready to start taking curative actions. You'll need to figure out exactly where your finances stand and what your cash flow situation looks like. With that information, you can begin to build your financial recovery plan. It will take time for your finances to bounce back, so be patient. As long as you keep taking action and moving forward, you will regain solid financial footing.

BOUNCE BACK FROM FINANCIAL DISASTER

Be a Financial Phoenix

No matter what caused your financial crash, there are specific steps you can take that will move you along the path from crisis to recovery. There is no quick fix here, though there are some things you can do quickly to set your financial recovery in motion. The trick is to start moving forward, to take the actions required to repair the damage, and defend your financial future.

One of the most important things to remember: you are not alone. Millions of people suffer and survive extreme financial setbacks and come out the other side with more financial strength and confidence than they had before. You can get through your crisis, regain control of your finances, and create a plan that will help make sure you never have to go through this again.

AVOID THE ROADBLOCKS TO RECOVERY

The biggest roadblock to financial recovery is you. Circumstances have wiped out your finances and left you in a miserable position where every decision seems overwhelming. Your emotions are all over the place—especially true when something you did (like extreme overspending or quitting your job before you had another one lined up) caused the financial upset.

Don't waste energy on guilt, shame, and blame. Beating yourself up over mistakes (real or perceived) can keep you from taking the steps you need to move forward. You'll need every bit of your emotional energy to solve your problems, face tough challenges, and stay motivated. Do what you can to reduce your stress and anxiety—yoga, deep breathing, therapy, whatever works.

Another common roadblock is coming up with a perfect plan. There's no such thing, so it's impossible to create it. Aiming for perfect can stop you from moving ahead at all. Make a plan, any plan that includes realistic action steps that will move your finances in the right general direction. You can make any fixes you need to along the way as long as you get started.

Remember: absolutely everyone (including me) has made a financial mistake or faced a major financial setback at some point. What's more important than how you got here is what you do next.

TAKE A NEW FINANCIAL INVENTORY

Whatever your financial situation was before the emergency, it's different now. That calls for a new financial inventory that reflects where things stand now. You need to know what resources you can count on, what obligations you face, and what additional setbacks might be looming in the months ahead. To do that, you need to gather up the same information you would to create a regular budget, and a little more on top of that.

- List your remaining assets
- Figure out how much money you owe
- Know how much monthly income you can count on
- Add up all of your necessary spending
- Check your credit score

- Find out potential financial consequences of the current situation (like tax liens or having your car repossessed, for example)

This first step is one of the most difficult because it forces you to look directly at your financial disaster. But knowing exactly where your finances stand right now and which things may affect your plans for financial recovery is the only way you can start fixing things.

SECURE YOUR HOME

If you're in danger of losing your home, take immediate steps to make sure that doesn't happen. This is not the same thing as making a choice to downsize or move somewhere more affordable; this is about avoiding eviction or foreclosure so you don't get kicked out of your house.

Once you've taken stock of your financial situation, you'll see right away if you'll be able to afford your current rent or mortgage payment during this temporary crisis. It you can't, inform your landlord or mortgage company right away. Be up front about your situation, reassuring the person you're dealing with that you have a plan to fix the problem and that you're already working on ways to get the money. It is much easier to negotiate for relaxed payment terms (like skipping a month, or making three small payments instead of one big payment) if you contact your landlord or mortgage company before you're late to pay.

If you can't make your next rent or mortgage payment, contact a HUD-approved housing counselor immediately to get free advice and counseling on how to avoid foreclosure or eviction. The Consumer Financial Protection Bureau website, www.consumerfinance.gov, has a searchable nationwide list of counselors to help you find a trustworthy resource. You can also call the Homeownership Preservation Foundation's HOPE hotline at 888-995-HOPE (4673). This independent nonprofit organization is dedicated to helping homeowners avoid foreclosure.

IF YOU'RE THINKING ABOUT FILING FOR BANKRUPTCY

During financial crises, many people think about filing for bankruptcy protection, and some feel as if it's their only option. In some cases, like if it's simply not possible for you to pay your debts, this may be the best choice. For many people, though, taking this route can do more damage than working through their financial setbacks. Plus, some people may not qualify for bankruptcy. Before you take any action in this direction, you need to know how the different kinds of bankruptcy work and understand the impact this will have on your financial future.

There are two types of bankruptcy for individuals: Chapter 7 and Chapter 13. Chapter 7 bankruptcy cancels most or all of your debts within six months. In return, you pay fees of about $350 and essentially turn over all of your assets and liabilities to the court. The court may sell off some of your property and make partial payments to your creditors. A Chapter 13 bankruptcy is more complicated and works sort of like a long-term repayment plan (it lasts three to five years). Most debts are not canceled under Chapter 13, though some unsecured debts (such as credit card debts) may be partially canceled.

Here are some other things you need to know about bankruptcy:

- You could lose your house if you file under Chapter 7.
- You'll still be responsible for 100 percent of some obligations such as child support, student loans, and tax debts, even with a Chapter 7 bankruptcy.
- Bankruptcy can't stop creditors from repossessing property linked to a secured debt (like your car if you can't pay your

auto loan), even after the debt is erased.

- Cosigners can (and usually will) get stuck with debts that you get out of under Chapter 7 (for example, if your mom cosigned for your car loan).
- You probably will have to ask permission before you can spend any of your own money under Chapter 13.
- Your credit score will plummet, and the bankruptcy can stay on your credit report for up to ten years.

Before you start bankruptcy proceedings, carefully weigh the pros and cons, and talk with a reputable credit counselor (you can find reliable counselors through the US Department of Justice at www.justice.gov) to learn about alternatives that might be better for your situation.

All the Ins and Outs of Bankruptcy

You can find credible and detailed information about both forms of bankruptcy, including which forms to file and step-by-step instructions on how to file, on the Nolo website at www.nolo.com.

CREATE AN EMERGENCY BUDGET

Set Your Spending to DEFCON 1

When a financial emergency strikes, you may need to toss out your regular budget temporarily. That's where an emergency budget comes in. Your emergency budget will help make sure that your emergency savings last as long as possible— especially if you don't have a steady income stream. That depends on three key factors: how much you have saved, how much you'll have to pull out every month, and when you expect to start bringing in steady (or additional) income.

Connect with a Support System

When you're going through a crisis, you need emotional support. If you're not comfortable sharing your situation with family and friends, join an online group for people in similar situations. Talk with a therapist to help you deal with the stress (you can find free or low-cost mental health services by visiting the Substance Abuse and Mental Health Services Administration at www.samhsa.gov). Reach out to someone to help you through the rough spots.

This leaner version of your money plan cuts expenses to the bone to give you some breathing room as you try to increase income enough to cover your normal expenses. That doesn't mean you shouldn't include any wants or fun in your budget. In fact, if you don't, you're less likely to stick with the plan, and that will slow down your progress toward prosperity. Pick one thing to (responsibly) splurge on; it will help reduce the stress of living on a bare-bones budget.

DEFINE PRESSING PRIORITIES

When your finances are in emergency mode, you'll need to prioritize your necessary expenses and prepare for the fact that they may not all get covered every month. This high-stress, temporary situation calls for drastic spending cuts until you're back on your full financial feet.

Your most important expenses will likely include:

- Housing (including utilities)
- Food
- Transportation
- Medical care
- Anything you need to get to work (like child care)
- One small splurge item (to help keep you on track)

If you're unable to cover all of those essentials, you'll need to make some hard choices. Rank them in order of importance, and pay for them in that order. Downsize any essential expense that you can, even if only temporarily (for example, find someone to carpool with or rent out a room). Use existing credit card rewards points to pay for necessities like basic groceries. See if you can find some ways to barter for what you need most (like driving a trusted neighbor to the airport in exchange for an hour of after-school child care).

FIND EXTRA MONEY ANYWHERE YOU CAN

The best way to make space in your budget is by seeking out any source of money available to you. You can try some of the income-boosting tips in Chapter 5. You can also use the following additional urgent funding sources while you're trying to generate some steady cash flow.

- Reduce your withholding taxes to increase your take-home pay (but know this can result in a higher tax bill going forward).
- Apply for unemployment insurance.
- Find out if you're eligible for food-based programs like the Supplemental Nutrition Assistance Program (SNAP) or Women, Infants, and Children (WIC) by visiting the USDA Food and Nutrition Service website at www.fns.usda.gov.
- Get any other federal or state government help you qualify for, such as energy assistance, Medicaid, and Children's Health Insurance Program (CHIP).
- Visit local food pantries to stock your fridge.
- Accept help from family and friends.

You may be hesitant, even ashamed, to use some of these options, but they exist for times just like these. They will help you get through the worst of it so you can work your way out of this temporary situation. Suck it up, fill out the applications, and move forward.

PARE EXPENSES DOWN TO THE BONE

With less (or no) money coming in, you'll need to make some drastic temporary budget cuts to reflect that current income. You'll need to eliminate every unnecessary expense so you can make whatever income you do have coming in and any savings that you have last as long as possible.

Unless an expense is an absolute necessity (food, housing, or medical care, for example) or needed to help you get back on your feet (such as a job-search related cost or networking opportunity), it does not have a place in this emergency budget. (The only exception: the single low-cost treat you've chosen to help yourself through.) Find ways to reduce your spending on necessities wherever possible, especially variable expenses like groceries and electricity.

Contact your creditors if you can't make your regular payments. Explain your situation, and ask them to temporarily reduce or suspend payments or extend due dates. The sooner you reach out to them, especially if it's before you stop making full (or any) payments, the more likely they'll be to cut you some slack.

Avoid the temptation to use credit cards to get through this period, especially for off-budget items. High-interest credit card debt will make it even harder to make ends meet in the months ahead.

KEEP INSURANCE TO PROTECT YOUR FINANCIAL FUTURE

Always Work with a Safety Net

Insurance is often one of the first expenses on the chopping block when people make budget cuts, but that is a wrong move. If something else happens—a fender bender, a burst appendix, a cracked pipe—you'll need the insurance to manage the extra costs. Chances are, those unexpected costs your insurance covers will be a lot bigger than your premium payments.

That said, you can look for ways to lower your premiums. Removing extra coverage and increasing deductibles will reduce your costs. You can also check in with your insurer to see if you qualify for any discounts (like going five years without a traffic ticket). Another possibility: ask your insurance company if they offer extended payment terms, such as making six smaller premium payments instead of two larger ones.

Figure out any way you can to keep your existing insurance policies active. They'll help protect you against additional financial losses, especially important when you're already struggling to make ends meet. Plus, you'll forfeit all the money you've already put into premiums this year if you let your policies lapse.

LIFE INSURANCE IS EVEN MORE CRUCIAL NOW

Think about this: if your family is having a hard time making ends meet, imagine how much harder it would be if a breadwinner died. Life insurance provides a critical safety net should the worst happen. This is not an expense to skip altogether, but you may be able to lower your premiums by making adjustments to your policy.

Make sure to maintain enough life insurance to cover a few years' worth of the income that would be lost without you, the balance of your mortgage, and all of the funeral costs.

DON'T DUMP YOUR HEALTH INSURANCE

Health insurance may seem like an unnecessary expense, especially when you're young and healthy. But it only takes one serious illness or injury to devastate your finances and your financial future. If your healthcare coverage costs more than you can afford, do your homework and shop around for a different plan. As expensive as health coverage can be, it still costs less than emergency care.

If you're healthy and don't have children, you can get away with high deductibles and catastrophic coverage. When kids are part of the picture or when you have ongoing health issues, you need more than bare-bones coverage.

When the financial setback is due to job loss, find out about your COBRA options. COBRA is a law designed to let people who've lost their jobs continue health coverage under the same plan for up to eighteen months. You'll have to foot the full bill for premiums, which may be expensive, but it may still cost less than getting an individual policy. Find out the details from your employer so you can make the best decision about health coverage for your family.

If none of these options work in your current situation, look into Medicaid eligibility before a health crisis comes up. You can find out more about this emergency health coverage at www.medicaid.gov.

Health Emergencies Can Kill Savings

Emergency healthcare is even more costly than most people realize. Check out these average costs for the most common emergency room visits:

- Sprains and strains: $1,498
- Open wounds: $1,650
- Kidney stones: $4,247
- Back problems: $1,476
- Intestinal infections: $2,398

KEEP YOUR CAR INSURANCE

In every state, it's illegal to drive an uninsured car, and the penalties for doing it can be severe and expensive. In most states, you'll have to pay hefty fines, and you could lose your driver's license or have your car registration revoked. You could even face jail time. And that's all if you get caught without having been in an accident.

If you cause an accident when you're uninsured, you will have huge out-of-pocket costs. Not only will you have to pay to get your own car fixed and cover your own medical bills (regular health insurance may not cover medical expenses due to accidents), but in most states you could also be sued by the other driver for that person's injuries and damages.

Bottom line: don't ditch your car insurance. Instead, trim this cost as much as you can by learning your state's minimum coverage requirements and adjusting your auto policy accordingly. You can find this information for every state on the GEICO website (www.geico.com).

REBUILD SAVINGS

Fill Up Your Piggy Bank

Restoring your savings, especially any retirement funds you had to dip into, is priority one once you've finally gotten through the rough patch. You'll need to replenish your financial safety nets before you can begin taking strides toward the goals you had to deprioritize during the crisis.

This doesn't mean just repaying yourself the money you took from savings. It also includes making up for skipped contributions (this may not be possible for certain retirement accounts). To bring your savings up to where they would have been if you hadn't experienced the emergency situation, and not just bring them back to where they were pre-crisis, add a reasonable amount for lost growth on to your makeup contributions. For example, if you skipped ten $100 deposits into savings, your account would be short $1,000 plus the interest that money would have earned. To catch up all the way, figure out how much interest you missed out on and include that in your makeup funds (the easiest way to do this is using an online savings calculator, which you can find at www.bankrate.com or www.investor.gov).

PAY BACK YOUR RETIREMENT ACCOUNT

If you borrowed from your retirement savings, it's critical to pay that money back as fast as you can. You've already lost out on some compounding (the earnings probably would have outpaced the interest you're paying yourself), but you don't want to lose even more growth opportunities. Time is your biggest advantage when it comes to long-term savings, so don't wait to refill your retirement nest egg.

If you borrowed money from your 401(k) and you're still working for the employer that holds your account, you've probably been paying that loan back through payroll deductions. Ask your employer to increase the payback amount so you can restore your savings faster. Plus, since many plans will not let you make contributions until your loan is paid in full, the sooner that's done, the sooner you can get back to building your retirement nest egg.

You Can't Borrow from an IRA

While you can take a loan from your 401(k) account, you can't borrow from an IRA. In fact, you can't even pledge your IRA as collateral on loan applications. Money you take out of a traditional IRA pre-retirement counts as a taxable early distribution.

Once you've paid yourself back, budget for the maximum allowable contributions going forward. That may include doubling up: if you have an employer-sponsored plan such as a 401(k), in most cases you can also open and contribute to an IRA (individual retirement account). Saving more aggressively might keep things a little tight right now, but you'll be very thankful when you're ready to retire and you have a substantial nest egg to rely on.

TACKLE NEW HIGH-INTEREST DEBT

It may seem counterintuitive to include debt paydown as part of a savings rebuild plan, but getting rid of debt with a high interest rate will do more for your overall financial picture than earning 2 percent on your emergency fund. Chances are, you relied on credit cards and other expensive options (like payday or personal loans) during your financial crisis. Focus your budget on paying them off to avoid rapidly growing compound interest charges. (Chapter 6 tackles debt paydown strategies in more detail.)

Once this new debt is paid off, you'll be able to quickly refill your savings accounts by shifting those debt payments directly into savings. And without the shadow of debt hanging over your finances, your money will have more room to grow.

REPLENISH YOUR EMERGENCY FUND

After you've refunded your retirement savings and gotten rid of high-interest debt, it's time to turn to rebuilding your emergency fund and making it bigger than it was before. Having that emergency savings buffer in place again will restore financial security and help you weather the next surprise more easily. This is one of those times when turning over couch cushions to hunt for change (literally and figuratively speaking) will move you more quickly toward your goal.

Whatever your emergency savings goal was before, consider doubling it. Look back on how quickly you ran through it when the last disaster struck. If you expected it to cover three months of expenses, did it? If your prior savings didn't stretch as far as you needed it to, you may have underestimated your crisis needs. Now you know how much it takes to get through a financial disaster, and you can make a better backup plan.

Take every opportunity to add to your emergency savings. Putting your change into a jar and then depositing the lot every week or two will start to add up faster than you'd expect. Programs such as Bank of America's Keep the Change round up debit card purchases to the nearest dollar and automatically transfer that "change" from your checking account into savings. Apps such as Digit (the app that randomly swipes little bits of money out of your checking account and into savings) can also help your savings move forward painlessly.

REVISIT YOUR SAVINGS GOALS

Now that you've gotten through the financial emergency, it's time to revisit your savings goals. You may find that some of the goals you set pre-crisis don't suit you anymore or have a different place among your priorities. Many people who've survived a sharp financial jolt like the one you've just lived through find that the things that matter to them now are very different than what seemed important before. Revised goals may include supersizing emergency savings, doubling up on retirement goals, and doing everything possible to avoid debt—but that can leave no room at all for fun goals (like vacations) that give you something to look forward to.

Take some time to think about your financial priorities. Review your SMART goals, and keep the ones that still fit. Create new goals that mesh with your new financial outlook. When you're ready, restart your goal-savings habit. And remember to strive for some fun.

REPAIR DAMAGED CREDIT

Get Your Cred Back

Bad credit can cost you money—and grief—in several ways, making it even harder to get your finances back on track. When your credit score comes back as fair or poor, you'll pay higher interest on any credit card or loan that you can get, making every dollar you borrow more expensive. On top of that, poor credit can keep you from getting a job, an apartment, utility hookup, and even life insurance.

Luckily, there's a lot you can do to quickly boost your credit score and continue to strengthen it over time. The most important thing to do going forward is to make every payment on time or risk seeing your credit score plummet again.

What's a Good Credit Score?

Credit scores can range from 300 to 850. Different lenders have slightly different guidelines when it comes to credit scores, but they generally consider scores above 700 to be good and scores over 750 to be excellent (according to Credit Karma).

VERIFY YOUR CREDIT REPORT IS CORRECT

You'd be surprised by how common it is to find mistakes on your credit report, and those mistakes can mess with your score. Getting errors off of your report takes minimal effort but gives you maximum returns by increasing your score quickly.

Start by ordering a copy of your credit report from each of the three major reporting agencies: Equifax, Experian, and TransUnion. You can get a free credit report every year at www.annualcreditreport.com or from each of the reporting agencies individually on their websites (www.equifax.com, www.experian.com, and www.transunion.com). Read through the full report carefully and highlight anything that's incorrect, which could include a charge that's not yours, a bill that's been paid, or ongoing activity in an account that you closed.

If you do find mistakes—and there's a good chance you will because at least 20 percent of all credit reports contain errors, according to the Federal Trade Commission (FTC)—notify one of the credit reporting agencies right away by certified mail (there's a good sample dispute letter along with a list of all the information you should provide on the Federal Trade Commission website at www.consumer.ftc.gov or at myFICO at www.myfico.com). Once you've reported the mistake, the credit reporting company has to open an investigation and notify the company that provided the inaccurate information. If that company agrees that the disputed data is inaccurate, the company has to notify all three credit reporting agencies so they can fix the mistake in your file.

GET CURRENT AND STAY CURRENT

To keep your credit score moving in the right direction, it's critical to fix any late payments you can and make all of your current payments on time. Late payments don't disappear from your credit report even when you close accounts—they linger for up to seven years—so do your best to avoid missing due dates. The most important thing here is to be proactive by contacting creditors before your account becomes seriously delinquent and sent to collections.

If you're struggling to pay all of your bills, there are ways to get help, including:

- HARP, the Home Affordable Refinance Program (www.harp.gov), for example, can help you refinance your mortgage to lower your monthly payment.
- American Water (www.amwater.com) is available in several states to provide financial assistance to people who need help paying their water bills.
- The Lifeline Program (www.usac.org/li/) can reduce phone or Internet costs (but not both).

Reducing payments anywhere you can, even temporarily, can help you avoid late payments and keep your credit score from tanking.

Ask for Forgiveness

If you've made only one or two late payments, ask your creditors to forgive them. They're more likely to say yes if you contacted them ahead of time to let them know you were undergoing a financial setback, but they may agree even if you didn't. Credit card companies especially are willing to forgive late payments for customers who had a good history of on-time payments before the problem appeared.

LOWER YOUR UTILIZATION

Another quick way to boost your credit score is by reducing your credit utilization, the amount of credit you're using compared to your total available credit. As long as your utilization is under 30 percent, it won't have a negative effect on your credit score; if it's over 30 percent, your score will drop.

Here's how it is calculated: if you have $15,000 in credit card debt and $25,000 in available credit, your credit utilization would equal 60 percent. The best way to reduce that ratio is to pay down your debt without racking up any new charges. You can also reduce it by increasing your available credit, but that can backfire if you end up charging more or if it requires another credit check.

When you're trying to increase your credit score, do not close any credit accounts once you pay them off. If it's a credit card payoff, stop using the card and strongly consider destroying it altogether—but don't cancel it. That will have the effect of increasing your utilization by reducing your available credit, the opposite of what you're trying to accomplish.

DON'T APPLY FOR ANY NEW LOANS

While you're working to improve your credit score, don't apply for any new loans, financing, or credit cards. Any time you do, the prospective lender will do a "hard pull," a credit check that indicates you've asked to borrow money. Every hard pull lowers your credit score, and those pulls stay on your credit report for about two years.

Multiple hard pulls in a short time period can send up red flags to the credit reporting agencies. They look at that as a sign you're planning to run up a lot of new debt, a bad idea when you're trying to increase your credit score.

RETURN TO YOUR REGULAR BUDGET

Back to Your Regularly Scheduled Program

Once you've gotten all the way through a financial disaster, you'll be able to start taking the necessary steps to bring your financial picture back to normal. You'll have more financial breathing room and be able to get back to your normal budget. While you're doing that, think about how you ended up having extreme money trouble in the first place. There may be areas of your old regular budget that need reshaping to help you prevent a money crisis the next time an emergency crops up.

REVISIT YOUR SPENDING TRIGGERS

When you're in emergency mode, survival instincts take over and behavior changes come almost automatically, sort of like "fight or flight" for your finances. Now that the immediate danger has passed, you can relax and get back to normal. But any behaviors that were around before—including the ones that contributed to your crisis—can resurface.

This is the time to revisit negative financial habits or spending triggers that can wreak havoc on your budget. Even if you had them under control before and during the crisis, they can creep back if you aren't looking for them. By facing these head on now, before they become problematic, you'll be able to avoid falling back into well-worn patterns that can stand in the way of your goals.

KEEP SOME CUTS TO GET AHEAD FASTER

While you were in the thick of your emergency budget, you made some extra expense cuts and probably got used to living without a lot of things that felt like needs before the crisis hit. Hanging on to some parts of your "lean" lifestyle can help make sure you don't ever suffer the same level of financial disaster again.

Think carefully before adding all of those cuts back into your budget. If there were things you found you could easily live without (such as professional pedicures or Takeout Tuesdays), don't go back to them. This doesn't mean you should stick with the full-on austerity budget; you shouldn't, and you should go back to spending on the things that matter to your life. But diving right back into old spending patterns that don't serve your goals could make it harder to weather the next financial storm.

PUT YOUR WEALTH-BUILDING PLANS BACK ON TRACK

Now that you've re-secured your finances and returned to your normal budget, it's time to get back to building up your wealth. The sooner you do this, the stronger your financial position will get, and that can help avoid financial meltdown if another crisis occurs. After you've built up sufficient savings, you can confidently turn your focus toward creating a substantial nest egg.

One of the best ways to increase your net worth is long-term investing in the stock market. If your budget doesn't have a lot of wiggle room, and minimum account balances topping $1,000 are currently out of reach, harness the power of apps like Acorns to send automatic micro contributions into personal investment accounts.

Invest for Purpose and Profit

Swell Investing offers microinvesting with a twist: social responsibility. Its portfolios focus on companies with growth potential and impact on the planet, with themes like renewable energy, clean water, and healthy living.

If you want to dip your toe into more focused investing, try apps such as the Robinhood and Stockpile apps that have no account minimums and let you buy stocks and exchange-traded funds without paying any brokerage fees or commissions (which would otherwise eat into your returns). The apps are easy to use, and they only take minutes to get started. And unlike other "fee-free" trading platforms, there are no hidden costs here. The trade-off is that their investment selection is limited (for example, you can't invest in mutual funds here), they don't offer research tools other than current market data, and they don't offer any retirement investment accounts.

Once your finances are in solid shape, you can expand your investing to more robust platforms with online brokerage firms like Vanguard (www.vanguard.com) and Charles Schwab (www.schwab.com). You'll have access to many more potential investments and more freedom to invest in your own style. To build a solid portfolio, you'll need to choose your investments wisely with a long-term focus and carefully balance risk (the chance that you'll lose money) and returns (potential profits).

It's usually easier to increase your income than cut expenditures. One way to raise some fast cash is having a yard sale, getting rid of old or little-used household objects.

Creating and maintaining a home budget doesn't have to be a burden, but it's a serious undertaking. Use a spreadsheet, software, or apps to create your budget and update it on a regular basis.

Eating out is fun and makes a nice break from routine. But it can also break your budget if you do it too often. Think about your eating habits and decide how big a part of your budget dining out is going to be.

College tuition for you or your children can be an enormous expense—one that gets larger every year. Start your budgetary planning early. To save big, consider attending a local community college for two years before switching to a four-year institution.

Travel can often be a big expense, but it doesn't have to wreck your finances. Plan your travel budget systematically, including the cost of transportation, food, housing, and sightseeing. If the expense is more than your budget can bear, wait a while until you've saved the amount of money you need.

Pets make our lives richer and more fun. They also impact our budgets. Your pet will need food and other supplies, as well as pet insurance and regular visits to the vet. Build all that into your household expenses.

Many people living paycheck to paycheck are tempted to take out payday loans. This isn't a good idea, since such lenders often charge exorbitant interest rates that can make it nearly impossible to get out of debt.

Selling your home is a big undertaking from a budgetary standpoint. Many people find it easier to make ends meet by downsizing to a smaller home with a lower mortgage payment and lower property taxes.

When two people decide to get married, they should review their finances—especially if they'll be merging their bank accounts. Many people also create a separate budget for the wedding itself.

A new baby is a huge event in your life. It also calls for a big budgetary overhaul. Examine the costs of housing, baby supplies, clothing, food, healthcare, and child care—preferably before the little one shows up in the delivery room.

As you enter retirement, your finances become dependent on savings, Social Security, and other income streams. Start planning early and create a budget plan that will support the retirement lifestyle you want.

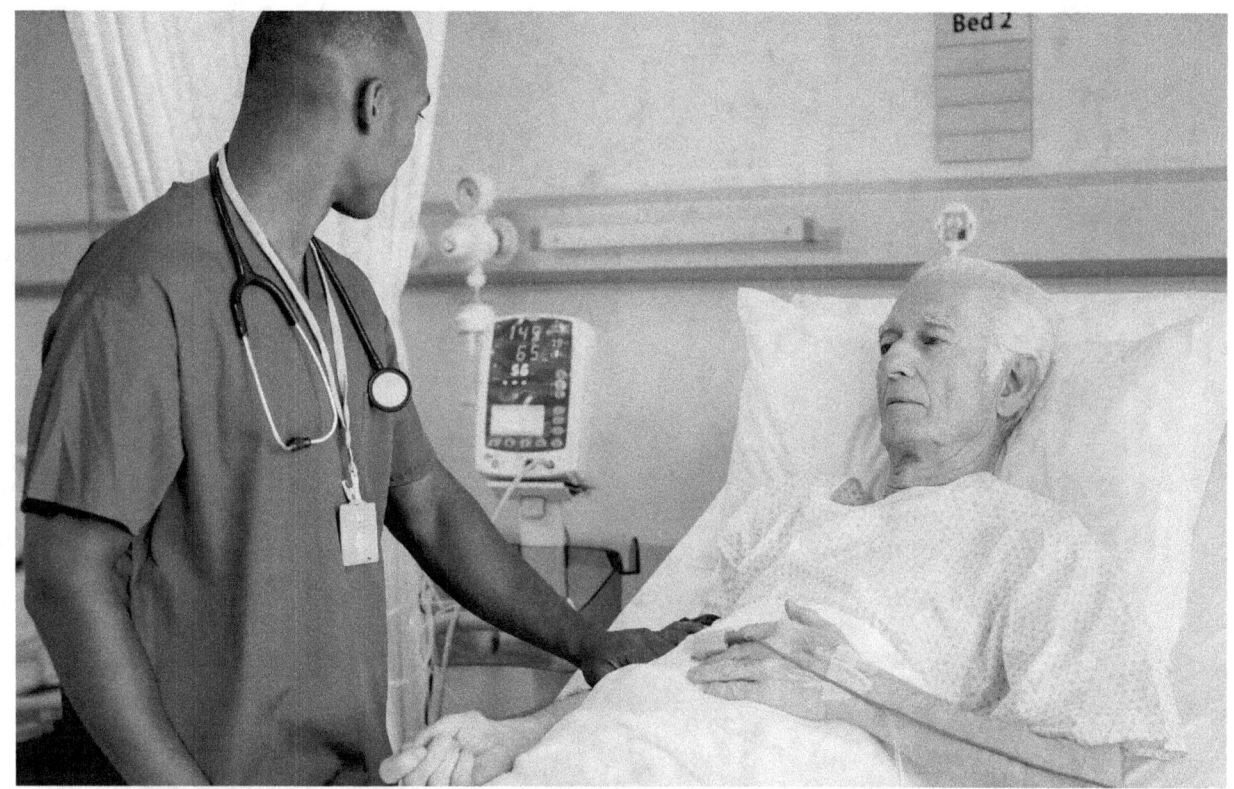

Healthcare becomes a significant element in budgets as we age. Not all medical expenses are covered by Medicare, and there are likely to be unexpected medical events. A realistic budget can ease the pain of these expenses.

One of the biggest purchases you may make in your lifetime is a car. When budgeting for a car purchase, remember to build in gas and regular maintenance. That way, your budget is less likely to encounter surprises down the road.

Good credit makes it easier to keep your finances on track. When you get your credit report, be sure to check it carefully, since up to 20 percent of reports contain errors.